DAILY ENCOURA(

COPYRIGHT ©2023

Jean P Erickson

All rights reserved. This book or any portion thereof may not be reproduced or used in any manner whatsoever without the express written permission of the publisher except for the use of brief quotations in a book review.

All Biblical references quoted from King James Bible

ISBN: 9798868483448
First Printing 2023
Contact email: jean.erickson1616@gmail.com
Or 5427denisemarie@gmail.com

Published by: DENISE MARIE DEMERS

365 Day Devotional...God still speaks today...John 10:27

DAILY ENCOURAGING WORDS...*TO LIVE BY*

DAILY ENCOURAGING WORDS
...to live by

365 DAY DEVOTIONAL
...with Scriptures

Author: JEAN P. ERICKSLON

John 10:27
My sheep hear my voice; I know them, and they follow Me.

Published by: DENISE-MARIE DEMERS

365 Day Devotional...God still speaks today...John 10:27

DAILY ENCOURAGING WORDS...*TO LIVE BY*

365 Day Devotional...God still speaks today...John 10:27

DAILY ENCOURAGING WORDS...*TO LIVE BY*

FORWARD
...BY JEAN ERICKSON

I have been changed with encouraging words since 2014 when I received this gift of scribing on my birthday...a gift of scribing through the Holy Spirit.
My life has been so different since I allowed the Holy Spirit within me to do a mighty work to transform me according to God's will...through encouraging words.
I would receive an unction beginning with "Arise and Shine for the Glory Light of Jesus has come"...hence a part of the title of this wonderful devotional.
Since receiving this gift, I have shared these encouraging "Words" with the multitudes through the internet and other media means.

There is power in God's word to change our lives and fulfill our destiny to the fullness that God has intended for us.
I dedicate this devotional to all who may read this so as your lives would change as you allow the Holy Spirit to do the work in you as He has done in me....be blessed!

365 Day Devotional...God still speaks today...John 10:27

DAILY ENCOURAGING WORDS...*TO LIVE BY*

DEDICATION

I first and foremost dedicate this devotional all in all to our Lord Jesus Christ...inspired and quickened in revelation and truth by the Holy Ghost...our Helper.

May this devotional edify, exhort, and encourage the reader for years to come.

May this devotional also, encourage others in the Body of Christ to seek the gift of Scribing for our Lord Jesus Christ.

Many, many people in this broken world are hurting and long to hear words of encouragement sometimes just to get through life...one day at a time.

Know that as we communicate with God through praise worship and genuine fellowship...God truly hears us and will respond through His Holy Spirit in that small still voice in our hearts that we learn to recognize as the voice of the Holy Ghost.

I also give special thanks in dedicating my gratitude to Denise-Marie Demers in helping me create and publish this devotional.

John 10:27
My sheep hear My voice, and I know them, and they follow Me:

365 Day Devotional...God still speaks today...John 10:27

DAILY ENCOURAGING WORDS...*TO LIVE BY*

JANUARY

Isaiah 43:19

Behold, I will do a new thing; now it shall spring forth; shall ye not know it? I will even make a way in the wilderness, and rivers in the desert.

365 Day Devotional...God still speaks today...John 10:27

DAILY ENCOURAGING WORDS...*TO LIVE BY*

January 1st

Arise and shine for the Glory Light of Jesus has come!
Rejoice in Me this day and let your spirit rise within you to let your voice be heard, praising Me and giving Me honor.
As you do this, the atmosphere around you will begin to feel light and full of joy as you create My strength to manifest in you.
For the joy of the Lord is your strength. It is My strength that carries you through rough times that comes into your life.
As you put your trust in Me and continue to praise Me, you will be in the Spirit and your everyday life will become the life you want to have.
I live within you; it is I that lives in you by My Holy Spirit.
You get stronger and stronger as you surrender to Me.
Give all to Me.
Go about your day and be blessed!

Exodus 15:2

The Lord is my strength and song, and He is become my Salvation. He is my God, and I will prepare Him an habitation, my Father's God and I will exalt Him.

DAILY ENCOURAGING WORDS...*TO LIVE BY*

January 2nd

Arise and shine for the Glory Light of Jesus has come.
I shine upon you this day so that you will be able to live your life with the power and presence of My Glory.
Let your heart be lifted in a song of praise and thanksgiving...the joy of your God bubbling up and out of your heart.
This pleases Me so that My children are going about their day rejoicing in Me.
As you do this, the people around you will feel My presence and will long to have what you have.
The Joy of the Lord is your strength, let continual praise come out of you the whole day.
Don't take your eyes off Me and see how your day will be. I am always with you...you are blessed!

Psalm 18:1-2

I will love thee, O Lord, my strength. The Lord is my rock, and my fortress and my deliverer, my God.
My strength in whom I will trust, my buckler, and the horn of my Salvation, and my High Tower.

DAILY ENCOURAGING WORDS...*TO LIVE BY*

January 3rd

Arise and shine for the Glory Light of Jesus has come!
Know that this day is a very special day.
The love of the Father flows through you and that love conquers all things!
There is nothing that the enemy of your soul can do against you, for My love is so great.
You walk in My love and by faith in Me.
Live your life Holy for I Am Holy.
You will live an overcomer's life.
Let the peace of God work in your life, and honor Me and praise Me.
You can walk in Me and have the life that I have planned for you right along.
Walk out your day and know you are blessed!

1st John 4:9

In this was manifested the love of God towards us because that God sent His only begotten Son into the world, that we might live through Him.

DAILY ENCOURAGING WORDS...*TO LIVE BY*

January 4th

Arise and shine for the Glory Light of Jesus has come!
Today let us walk hand in hand down the pathway of life, as we work together.
We can conquer anything that will revolt against you this day.
If you put Me first and give all to Me, My strength and power will overtake you and you will be able to handle anything in your way.
The Joy of the Lord is your strength.
Lift your voice and praise Me, as you do this My Joy will flood your whole being.
You will see what your God can do in your life. You need not walk alone and always be downcast and lonely.
So let us walk together and you will become the overcomer that I see you to be. I love you...go about your day.

Isaiah 41:10

Fear not, for I am with thee; be not dismayed, for I am they God. I will strengthen thee, yea, I will help thee; yea I will uphold thee with the right hand of My Righteousness.

365 Day Devotional...God still speaks today...John 10:27

DAILY ENCOURAGING WORDS...*TO LIVE BY*

January 5th

Arise and shine for the Glory Light of Jesus has come!
Look to Me the Author and Finisher of your faith.
As you turn your life over to Me and trust Me to work in your life, to establish your faith.
As you grow from Glory to Glory, your faith becomes stronger. Without faith you cannot please Me.
This is why you cannot walk with Me without faith.
As you trust Me and put your life into My hands, I walk with you and together we will walk the good fight of faith.
I never intended for you to walk your life out by yourself.
As things come your way, look to Me for the answer.
You are putting your faith in Me, and faith is what moves My Hand to move in your life for the answer.
I love you with everlasting love and I will never leave you or forsake you. Take My Hand and never let go!

Hebrews 12:2
Looking unto Jesus the author and finisher of our faith, who for the joy that was set before him endured the cross, despising the shame, and is set down at ...

365 Day Devotional...God still speaks today...John 10:27

DAILY ENCOURAGING WORDS...*TO LIVE BY*

January 6th

Arise and shine for the Glory Light of Jesus has come!
Walk in the goodness of your God. Did you not see the Hand of your God work on your behalf this day?
You stood firm believing that I would give you favor, you believed and received what you wanted Me to do on your behalf.
That is the way that I want all My children to do.
Stand in faith believing and receiving what you wanted from Me.
I am always waiting for My children to learn how to walk in this faith, not only today but every day.
It is a way of life, that is the Kingdom way, and it will never fail.
It is built on faith and faith will never let you down.
So, build up your faith each and everyday and use it to the fullest!

Mark 11:24
Therefore, I say unto you, what things soever ye desire, when ye pray, believe that ye receive them, and ye shall have them.

January 7th

Arise and shine for the Glory Light of Jesus has come!
Be not dismayed for I am with you.
I am working in your life to change what is needed to bring you to the place of maturity in Me.
There is a lifetime of events that have caused you to be the way that you are.
Keep surrendering your life to Me.
I am the only one that knows your heart and I am the only one to change you if you are willing.
All things work together for good, because I am good, and I see the potential in you and your willingness to have Me do the work in you to bring about change.
Then and only then, you will be able to do the work I have called you to do.
I can only go as far as you will let Me.
We can achieve this goal together.
Put your faith in Me, praise, and worship Me.
I am moved by the praises of My children unto Me.
That is where the power is, and, by faith.
All things are done by faith in Me and the work of the cross.

Psalm 37:5
Commit your way unto the Lord, trust also in Him, and He shall bring it to pass.

DAILY ENCOURAGING WORDS...*TO LIVE BY*

January 8th

Arise shine for the Glory Light of Jesus has come!
Be still and know that I AM is your God.
Rely on Me for whatever you need for this day.
My ears are open to hear you when you call out My name.
I am ever so near to you.
I long to hear the cries of My people.
Call in faith believing, and I will answer you.
I long to bless My children.
Know that whatever you need or want, I can, and I will fulfill it.
I don't want My children walking in lack, but to be walking in the full Blessing in every part of their lives.
You are made in the likeness of Me, and I am not poor in any sense of the word, nor do I live in lack.
I am all powerful and there is nothing I don't have, and all things are possible with Me.
So, tell Me what is on your heart and believe with all your heart and see the Hand of the Lord move on your behalf.

Philippians 4:6
Be careful for nothing, but in everything by prayer and supplication with thanksgiving, let your request be made known unto God!

DAILY ENCOURAGING WORDS...*TO LIVE BY*

January 9th

Arise and shine for the Glory Light of Jesus has come!
Be not dismayed My child for I am with you.
There is nothing you can't handle for you have the power within you to do all with all things.
I can do all things for greater is I that is in you, that he that is in the world.
You are to ask the Holy Spirit to help you, for that is where your strength comes from.
You are not meant to do things by yourself.
When you think you can do it in your own strength, that is where you get yourself into trouble.
Take heart My child and know that I am always waiting for you to ask Me to help you.
I will show you what to do. Because I have all the answers.
Rely on Me.
Do not let Satan steal your joy, for My Joy is your strength.
Look to Me and know that all is well.

Philippians 4:13
I can do all things through Christ, which strengthened me.

DAILY ENCOURAGING WORDS...*TO LIVE BY*

January 10th

Arise and shine for the Glory Light of Jesus has come!
Let My Glory Light penetrate your whole life.
When you walk in My light you are walking in My presence and all that I AM.
When your life is consumed with My presence, there is nothing that is withheld from you.
Whatever you ask in My name, I will do for you.
When you live in My presence and release your faith, there is nothing more powerful. You can walk in My presence 24/7.
To do this you have to leave your past behind and give up everything and let the Holy Spirit take over your life to follow the things of Me.
The Holy Spirit will lead you and teach you truth.
When you give your all to Him, you will have a life that will fulfill and sustain you everyday of your life.
I am always there to guide you through the rough times and the good times.
I am your God...trust Me!

Philippians 1:6
Being confident of this very thing, that He which hath begun a good work in you, will perform it until the day of Jesus Christ.

DAILY ENCOURAGING WORDS...*TO LIVE BY*

January 11th

Arise and shine for the Glory Light of Jesus is come!
Walk into My goodness this day.
Praise Me and expect to see the hand of God move in your life today. I have great things in store for you.
Continue to be in My word and fill yourself with My Word and it will bring forth these great things for you.
Stand firm and believe with all your heart, what the Word says for it is truth, walking out your life by the written Word.
Then you are walking in Me as I AM the Word, from the beginning I was the Word.
I took on flesh and blood and body so that I could die on the cross for the sins of the world.
I rose on the third day and now I sit at the right hand of the Father in Heaven.
It is important to learn My Word and do what it calls you to do.
Once you do this, your whole life will come alive, and you will begin to see the power and strength that comes from My Word to help you to become an overcomer in through Me.

John 1:11

...and the Word was made flesh, and dwelt among us, and we behold His Glory, the Glory as of the only begotten of the Father, full of Grace and truth.

365 Day Devotional...God still speaks today...John 10:27

DAILY ENCOURAGING WORDS...*TO LIVE BY*

January 13th

Arise and shine for the Glory Light of Jesus has come!
Take hold of My Mercy and Grace for this day.
They are new every morning.
Expect to see new things happen for you this day.
Look to Me and keep your eyes on Me, for I AM the one
that leads you and helps you in all that you do.
Ask of Me, believe and receive what you have asked for.
My Hand is opened unto you. Walk in faith and you will
have what you asked for.
My hand is opened unto you.
Pray My will and ask not amiss for all will be answered that is
prayed for according to My Will.
I long to bless My children.
So, allow Me to take you up higher in your prayer life.
Trust in Me, praise Me and walk in the Goodness of your
God this day!

James 1:6
*But let him ask in faith, nothing wavering. For he that
wavereth is like a wave of the sea, driven with the wind and
tossed.*

365 Day Devotional...God still speaks today...John 10:27

January 14th

Arise and shine for the Glory Light of Jesus has come!
Wait on Me, do not go before Me.
This is where you get into trouble.
When you do, this is where it drains your faith in Me.
You think that I AM not capable enough to know what the answer is to what has come up against you.
My child, do you not know the Creator of this world and all things in it and around it, has all the answers to every situation that would arise in anyone's life?
I am the one who put the plan in your life into motion, long before you were born.
You are My child and I love you very much.
Does not My Word say that you need not worry about things and that I would take care of all your needs?
Do not go back to the old ways to solve your problems, but reach out to Me, and stand in faith that your God will show you the answers to your problem.
In doing so it will increase your faith.
You cannot receive all from Me, without walking in faith, and stand on My Word, so that all will come forth.

Psalms 50:15
...and call upon Me in the day of trouble; I will deliver thee, and thou shall glorify Me.

DAILY ENCOURAGING WORDS...*TO LIVE BY*

January 15th

Arise and shine for the Glory Light of Jesus has come!
Come and dine, for I have set the table before you, so that you will be able to eat and be filled.
As you partake of Me, you will be full and then you will be able to help others in time of need.
You can not give out what you do not have yourself.
I have given all that you need.
You in turn must believe and take that which I have already prepared for you.
You need to be always filled with My Holy Spirit for the things that may come against you are more powerful than you are.
If you are not equipped by the Holy Spirit to fight against them, put Me first and continually keep your eyes on Me and allow My Holy Spirit to equip you and you will be strong and be an overcomer.

Psalms 23;5

Thou preparest a table before me in the presence of my enemies, Thou anointest my head with oil, my cup runneth over.

365 Day Devotional...God still speaks today...John 10:27

DAILY ENCOURAGING WORDS...*TO LIVE BY*

January 16th

Arise and shine for the Glory Light of Jesus has come! Do you not see the goodness and faithfulness of the power of you God that has been working in your life over the past few months?

Even though you seem to have been overtaken by the enemy of your soul and have been blinded to the point where you have been listening to his lies; My child it is very important for you to understand that the way of Satan is to shut you down and to destroy your life.

but I have come to give you life and keep you on the path of life that will see you through to the end of your destiny.

So, My child take hold of your thoughts and your tongue. Let them both line up with My Word and you will not waver in your walk with Me.

Learn to trust Me in all things and listen to My Holy Spirit's voice that is within you.

Draw close to Me and all Me to lead you and guide you.

John 10.10

The thief cometh not, but for to steal, and to kill, and to destroy: I am come that they might have life, and that they might have it more abundantly.

365 Day Devotional...God still speaks today...John 10:27

DAILY ENCOURAGING WORDS...*TO LIVE BY*

January 17th
Arise and shine for the Glory Light of Jesus has come!
Look to Me, the Author and Finisher of your faith.
All the things you need is in Me.
I see everything that goes on in your life.
Open your heart and tell Me what is on your heart, so that I can help you come to the place that you need to be.
That is on the top and not on the bottom of life.
My plan for you is a life that is meaningful and filled with Joy, Peace, and Love.
So, open to Me and give Me all things that would hold you down.
Start to praise Me and let My Glory fill you up and it will put you on the path that will lead you to Me and give you the power to overcome.
Always look to Me and give praise to the One who loves you with an everlasting love!

Jeremiah 31:3
The Lord hath appeared of old unto me, saying,
Yea, I have loved thee with an everlasting love; therefore, with lovingkindness have I drawn thee.

DAILY ENCOURAGING WORDS...*TO LIVE BY*

January 18th

Arise and shine for the Glory Light of Jesus has come!
My child today is a brand-new day.
I long to bless you and give you all that your heart desires.
I do not stop the flow, but I can not cross your will, so be
willing to open and let Me do what I always wanted to do.
I have planted deep things in you, and they must be worked
out in your life, so that all will come forth and you will become
the person I have already created.
You cannot stay in one place, because you walk in a spiritual
walk.
In the Spirit world, it is always moving.
If your walk in Me is not moving, you will miss out on
everything I have for you.
So, My child, choose to follow after Me and walk fully in
My ways for there is no other way!

Psalms 143:10
Teach me to do thy will, for thou (art) my God; thy Spirit
(is) good. Lead me into the land of uprightness.

DAILY ENCOURAGING WORDS...*TO LIVE BY*

January 19th
Arise and shine for the Glory Light of Jesus has come!
Today is a brand-new day in your life.
Expect great things to happen today.
You serve the King of Kings and Lord of Lords.
Nothing is too great or too small for Me to handle for you.
Ask Me and expect to receive from Me.
Every part of your life is an interest to Me.
I long to have you walk with Me all your days.
There is nothing that I have not provided so that you can walk out your life in victory.
All that you need is in Me.
Spend time in My word and presence so that I can make you the person I want your to be.
Come My child and sit at My feet and learn of Me!

1st Corinthians 15:57
But thanks be to God, which giveth us the Victory through our Lord Jesus Christ.

DAILY ENCOURAGING WORDS...*TO LIVE BY*

January 20th

Arise and shine for the Glory Light of Jesus has come!
They that wait upon the Lord shall renew their strength.
My strength is sufficient for you.
My power is within you.
All you must do is learn to tap into it.
That is done by faith believing that the Holy Spirit is the one that releases My power to you.
When you walk in My strength, you are walking in My Joy, My Power.
These are the weapons that destroy the power of the enemy.
You do not fight against flesh and blood but against wickedness in high places, so you cannot fight in your own strength.
So, prepare yourself spiritually and walk in My strength.
Always look to Me for I am always with you.
Stand firm and fight the good fight of Faith!

Ephesians 6:13
Therefore, take unto you the whole armor of God, that ye may be able to withstand in the evil day, and having done all, stand.

DAILY ENCOURAGING WORDS...*TO LIVE BY*

January 21st
Arise and shine for the Glory Light of Jesus has come!
Look not to yourself for the answers you need for your life.
Do not struggle and look for other ways to work out your own life.
Look to Me for the help and strength that you need.
I ask you to give all your troubles to Me, for My ways are not hard.
Cast all your cares on Me for I careth for you.
I love you and I long for you to lay down all your burdens and trust Me in all the things that you struggle with.
As you learn to do this, you will begin to feel the load lift off you.
You will be able to feel My Peace, Joy, and Love growing in your heart again.
You will walk with a spring in your step and your head held up high...that is what I want for you.
I will never leave you and I love you.
You are Blessed!

Mathew 1:29
Take My yoke upon you, and learn of Me, for I AM meek and lowly in heart and ye shall find rest into your soul.

365 Day Devotional...God still speaks today...John 10:27

DAILY ENCOURAGING WORDS...*TO LIVE BY*

January 22nd

Arise and shine for the Glory Light of Jesus has come!
Press into Me this day.
I do not only meet all your needs, but I also am your Healer.
The stripes on My back were taken for all the sickness and diseases.
By My stripes you are healed.
By faith you can walk in heath.
Believe and receive all that I have done on the Cross for you.
You need not walk in defeat for it was ALL done on the Cross.
The power of the resurrection of Christ has set all of mankind free. I have done it all for you.
I love you and My creation and I long for everyone to be whole in Me.
Receive, receive all that I have done for you.
You can walk in freedom and enjoy all your life in Me.
Put your life in My hands and be Blessed!

Isaiah 53:5

But He was wounded for our transgressions, He was bruised for our inequities, the chastisement of our peace was upon Him, and by His stripes...we are healed.

365 Day Devotional...God still speaks today...John 10:27

DAILY ENCOURAGING WORDS...*TO LIVE BY*

January 23rd

Arise and shine for the Glory Light of Jesus has come!
I have chosen you to walk with Me and I have called you to walk out your life in the power and strength that comes from Me.
I know the plans I have for you; they are good and not for evil.
Your life is written in My book of Life.
I watch over you and I live within you.
I walk close to you everyday of your life.
My love for you is everlasting and does not waiver.
There is nothing that I will not do if you ask in faith believing that I will do it for you.
I want to bring you to a place in Me that you will not put your trust in your own ability but put your trust in Me and never look back.
I am a NOW God, and you must walk in the now with Me.
Together we will accomplish what My will for your life is to be.
I will never leave you...you are Blessed this day!

Romans 8:28

And we know that all things work together for good to those who love God, to them who are the called according to His purpose.

DAILY ENCOURAGING WORDS...*TO LIVE BY*

January 24th

Arise and shine for the Glory Light of Jesus has come!
Be still and know that I am God.
Let your mind be centred towards Me.
Put aside all the thoughts that are not of Me.
Reign them in and put them under my Blood.
My Blood will wash away all things that do not line up with what is not giving Me all the Honor and Glory that belongs to Me.
Always be on guard of your mind for what you think about will surely take over and you will do that very thing.
Your mind is very powerful, you have My power within you to put down and get rid of every thought that does not line up with My Word, My will.
I have given you the tools to work with, My Name, My Blood, and My Authority, so use them against the enemy (Satan) that wants to take you off your walk with Me.
So, I say, walk in My light that goes before you, and as you do your part, I will do mine.

1st Thessalonians 5:21
Prove all things, hold fast that which is good.

DAILY ENCOURAGING WORDS...*TO LIVE BY*

January 25th

Arise and shine for the Glory Light of Jesus has come!

When you settle your mind and look to Me, I AM always there for you.

When the line of communications is open between you and Me, I will be able to show you how to handle your life the way it should be done.

I know what would happen in your everyday life.

Lean into Me and keep your heart and mind centered on Me.

You can do that if you are looking to Me.

I AM your strength and your helper in times of need.

When you are thinking about My ways, you will walk in My Peace and Joy.

You will be able to live your life pure and unclouded of the things of this world.

I called you out of this world and called you into a life of Holiness.

You are to be Holy for I am Holy, a life set apart for My Kingdom.

You live in this world, but you are not part of this world.

Continue to learn of My ways and you will be fulfilled!

John 17:16

They are not of this world, even as I am not of this world.

DAILY ENCOURAGING WORDS...*TO LIVE BY*

January 26th

Arise and shine for the Glory Light of Jesus has come!
I have given you the Holy Spirit to empower you to do all that you are called to do for Me.
You are chosen for the work of the Kingdom to be done on this earth.
I have called you to live a Holy life unto Me, so that my power can live in you and then and only then can you fill your calling on this earth.
I AM coming soon, and I AM looking for faith on the earth.
So, let your faith rise and take all I have for you.
You can not do this in your own strength, only by My strength.
Cast all your burdens on Me for I AM is your burden bearer.
Take My Yoke upon you for it is light.
Let My Holy Spirit lead you and guide you into all truth.
You are not called to walk alone...walk with Me!

Matthew 11:30
For My Yoke is easy, and My burden is light.

365 Day Devotional...God still speaks today...John 10:27

DAILY ENCOURAGING WORDS...*TO LIVE BY*

January 27th

Arise and shine for the Glory Light of Jesus has come!
Let go and let Me have My way in you.
When you hold onto things that have no Spiritual meaning to it, it only keeps you from having all that I long to give you.
The things of this world only keeps you from a life that would truly be worth living.
A life of peace and joy, not a life of chaos.
You must choose which way you are going to live.
You cannot live in both the world and walk a Spiritual life in Me.
The flesh and the Spirit Life cannot coincide together.
I call you to a higher walk of life.
It takes a surrendering of every part of your life.
If you work with Me, you will obtain a life that is filled with every good thing.
I died so that you could have all...I paid the price for you.
Receive all that is yours!

Romans 12:1
I beseech you therefore, brethren by the mercies of God, that ye present your bodies a living sacrifice, Holy, acceptable unto God. (which is) your reasonable service.

365 Day Devotional...God still speaks today...John 10:27

DAILY ENCOURAGING WORDS...*TO LIVE BY*

January 28th

Arise and shine for the Glory Light of Jesus has come!
Walk into My goodness this day.
Praise Me and expect to see the Hand of your God move in your life today. I have great things in store for you.
Continue to be in My Word and fill yourself with the Word and it will come alive in you in all areas of your life.
Stand firm and believe with all your heart, what the Word says for it is truth.
Walking out your life by the written Word, then you are walking in Me.
For I am the Word from the beginning...I was the Word.
I took on the flesh and blood body so that I could die on the Cross for the sins of the world.
I rose on the third day and now I sit at the right hand of the Father in Heaven.
It is important to learn My Word and do what it calls you to do.
Once you do this, your whole life will come alive, and you will begin to see power and strength that comes from My Word, and you become and overcomer in Me.

John 1:14

And the Word was made flesh, and dwelt among us, and we behold His Glory, the Glory as of the Grace and Truth.

365 Day Devotional...God still speaks today...John 10:27

DAILY ENCOURAGING WORDS...*TO LIVE BY*

January 29th

Arise and shine for the Glory Light of Jesus has come!
Take time to be in My presence for that is where you will find the strength and power to live out your day.
Each day is different; therefore, you need to do this daily.
You will then be able to deal with all the things that come at you in the run of the day.
Remember to keep your eyes on Me, so that you will be strong, and you will know that I will show you the way to go and you will not fear as there is no fear in Me.
Your faith will be in Me knowing that I will never fail you, nor will I mislead you.
Always putting My word in you.
You cannot live your life in Me if you do not know My Word and learn to live by My Word.
Speak it forth into your life.
As you do this you will become strong, and you will live out your life the way I called you to do.

Proverbs 4:20
My son, attend to My Words, incline thine ear into My sayings.

DAILY ENCOURAGING WORDS...*TO LIVE BY*

January 30th

Arise and shine for the Glory light of Jesus has come!
For those that have a hard time to walk in the Spirit are those that struggle with the flesh.
There is a time you as a child of God must decide to surrender everything to Me, so that I can work in your life, to bring you into the walk of the Holy Spirit.
That is to always walk with the Holy Spirit.
First thing on waking up in the morning, you need to ask My Holy Spirit what He wants you to do in your day.
Create your day walking in the Holy Spirit and not in the flesh.
When you walk in the Holy Spirit, you will become aware of things that are happening around you.
He will quicken to you what you need to do.
You are always battling with the enemy of your soul.
Satan will always try to trip you up and get you off guard so again it is important to always walk with the Holy Spirit.
He is your helper and will lead you in all truth!

Zechariah 1:6
Then he answered and spoke unto me saying, this is the Word of the Lord unto Zerubbabel, say, not by might, nor by power, but by My Spirit saith the Lord of Hosts.

365 Day Devotional...God still speaks today...John 10:27

DAILY ENCOURAGING WORDS...*TO LIVE BY*

January 31st

Arise and shine for the Glory Light of Jesus has come!
I have come so that you can have a life and have it more abundantly.
I gave My life on the Cross so that you would be able to live a life full of power, joy, peace, and love.
You would not have to live in lack, sickness or loneliness, or anything that would be negative in your life.
Everything that I died for is available this day.
I long to see you living a life full of My Goodness.
Give Me all that holds you down...sickness, pain, loneliness, lack of finances, and I will turn your life around.
Just come to me.
Surrender all these things to Me and take My Love and My ways of living a good and prosperous life.
I long to see My children living in victory and enjoying their life in Me.

Psalm 16;11
Thou wilt shew me the path of life, in thy presence (is) fulness of joy, at thy right hand. (there are) pleasures for evermore.

DAILY ENCOURAGING WORDS...*TO LIVE BY*

FEBRUARY

John 3:16

For God so loved the world, that he gave his only begotten Son, that whosoever believeth in him should not perish, but have everlasting life.

DAILY ENCOURAGING WORDS...*TO LIVE BY*

February 1st
Arise and shine for the Glory Light of Jesus has come!
Today is a great day of rejoicing.
Lift your head and sing unto your God.
Sing praises into Me.
Expect the unexpectable.
Do you not think that I AM cannot turn things around in your life and put things in order for you?
There is nothing that I do not see going on in your life that I cannot work out on your behalf.
Look to Me and know that our God is all sufficient.
Draw strength from Me this day and do not look back, don't look ahead but look to Me and I will lead you and guide you and put your feet on a straight and narrow path that will bring Glory to Me.
I love you My child.... all is well.

2nd Corinthians 12:9
...and He said unto me, My grace is sufficient for thee: for My strength is made perfect in weakness

DAILY ENCOURAGING WORDS...*TO LIVE BY*

February 2nd

Arise and shine for the Glory Light of Jesus has come!
As you put your life into My hands and surrender all to Me,
I will change you and you will see the changes in your life as you walk in Me.

You are notable to change yourself.

The power of the Holy Spirit within you works with you as you surrender daily to Him, and as you praise Me and give Me honor, you will begin to feel stronger.

It is a way of living from day to day.

Know that I AM with you every moment of the day and night.

When you are down, give it all to Me.

Rely on My strength to carry you through.

Do not hang on to anything.

Surrender all to Me.

I love you My child and I will see you through.

2nd Corinthians 3:18

But we all, with open face beholding as in a glass, the Glory of the Lord, are changed into the same image from Glory to Glory, even as by the Spirit of the Lord.

365 Day Devotional...God still speaks today...John 10:27

DAILY ENCOURAGING WORDS...*TO LIVE BY*

February 3rd

Arise and shine for the Glory Light of Jesus has come.
Look unto Me, the Author and Finisher of your faith.
As you turn your life over to Me and allow Me to work in your life; I will change your life so that I will begin to be seen in your life.
I change you from Glory to Glory.
It is a process, as you give to Me the things that hold you back.
Then in return I will put into you the things that will honor Me.
Be not afraid to let go but trust Me that I will do what I have said.
As you surrender all to Me, you are becoming an overcomer.
That is My goal for you, to be an overcomer in Me.
I will lead you and guide you in all things.
Put your trust in Me My child.

Romans 8:37
Nay, in all these things we are more than conquerors through Him that loved us.

DAILY ENCOURAGING WORDS...*TO LIVE BY*

February 4th

Arise and shine for the Glory Light of Jesus has come!
Go forth in the power and might of your God.
There is nothing that cannot be done, by faith through believing in the name of Jesus.
Jesus is the Name above all other names, everything must bow to the name of Jesus.
Through the resurrection of Jesus, you have the power within you to overcome all things.
I say to you this day to walk in Me and do so many great things for My Kingdom.
You no longer live to yourself, so let My will be done in you so you will be able to go forth and do mighty things for Me.
You need not fear, for greater is He that is within you than he that is in the world.
It is time to go forth and show the world that you are full of My power and might!
I've called you to be great for Me in this dying world.
Reach out and touch people in your surroundings.
I am with you and guide you all the way.

Colossians 3:17
...and whatsoever ye do in word, or deed, do all, in the name of the Lord Jesus, giving thanks to God and the Father by Him.

February 5th

Arise and shine for the Glory Light of Jesus has come!
Come and sit before Me, when you are weary, and I will strengthen you.
Put aside all things that seem to weigh you down.
Let your mind get quiet and just sit in My presence.
Let Me flow through you and I will touch every part of you.
When you sit quietly before Me, then I can pour into you, and you will begin to feel the strength come back into your being.
You are not equipped to handle all the things that come at you in the run of the day.
You can only withstand the things that come against you in My strength not yours, nor can you attempt to figure things out in your own mind.
Surrender all and rely on Me in everything.
I want to bring you to a place where you will totally trust Me in all things.
Let your faith rise and take over your life.
Ask Me to be at the helm of your ship, every moment of your day.

Jerimiah 31:25
For I have satiated the weary soul, and I have replenished every sorrowful soul.

DAILY ENCOURAGING WORDS...*TO LIVE BY*

February 6th

Arise and shine for the Glory Light of Jesus has come!
Walk in My presence, for I AM always with you.
In My presence is the fullness of Me, nothing is left out.
That is why you must train yourself to let go of all other
things that are of the flesh and of the world.
You have become a new creature in Me.
Does My word not say that old things have become new?
Let go of the past and embrace the new.
You will change from Glory to Glory.
Allow Me to work with you and walk with you on this journey
of life that I have ordained for you.
You were never meant to do all alone.
So put your hand into Mine and we will do it together.
Trust in Me all the way!

2nd Corinthians 5:17

Therefore, if any man be in Christ, he is a new creature: old things are passed away, behold, all things are become new.

DAILY ENCOURAGING WORDS...*TO LIVE BY*

February 7th
Arise and shine for the Glory Light of Jesus has come!
Rejoice, rejoice in Me this day, for I see all that is happening in your life.
Let not your heart be troubled for your God goes before you, working on your behalf.
Never forget that I AM always with you.
I know your thoughts even before you think them.
I am the all-knowing God.
Put Me at the helm of your life and trust me.
I have nothing but good things for your life.
Put your hand into My Hand and never look back.
Always looking forward, for I want you to be always moving forward, trusting Me and praising Me for all things.
I love you with an everlasting Love.

Hebrews 13:5
Let your conversation be without covetousness; and be content with such things as ye have for he hath said, I will never leave thee, nor forsake thee.

DAILY ENCOURAGING WORDS...*TO LIVE BY*

February 8th

Arise and shine for the Glory Light of Jesus has come!
Put away your thoughts and concentrate on what I have for you.
Lean not on your own understanding but ask of Me.
Follow My voice and you will not be lead astray.
I have great things in store for you.
I give you the strength to leave all behind, that would cause you to be weary.
My way is not troublesome.
My way will lead you into truth and My light will guide you on your journey of life.
Trust Me and press into Me.
Give all praise, honor, and Glory to Me.
Let your voice praise Me in song and thanksgiving.
Go about your day for you are blessed!

Proverbs 3: 5-6

Trust in the LORD with all thine heart, and lean not unto thine own understanding. In all thy ways acknowledge him, and he shall direct thy paths.

DAILY ENCOURAGING WORDS...*TO LIVE BY*

February 9th

Arise and shine for the Glory Light of Jesus has come!
As you spend time in My presence, you allow Me to minister to your spirit and soul, to strengthen you.
Everyday is a new day in Me.
I see what is in your day, but you do not until it is upon you.
That is why it is so important to allow Me to fill you up.
Take the time and let all other things go.
Nothing matters except what I have for you.
My presence is everything you need to conquer everyday duties and unexpected things.
I am there in every moment of your day.
Just call on My Name and draw from My Holy Spirit.
Make Me your priority and trust Me.
Let Me be on your mind first thing in the morning and the last thing on your mind at night.
You will become stronger and stronger in Me.

1st Chronicles 16:11
Seek the Lord and His strength, seek His face continually.

DAILY ENCOURAGING WORDS...*TO LIVE BY*

February 10th

Arise and shine for the Glory Light of Jesus has come!
Come unto Me and I will give you rest.
When you are weary, and your mind seems overwhelmed and cannot work the way that I have created to work.
Stop and surrender all to Me.
Learn to lean into Me and let Me take over to let My Holy Spirit settle your mind.
Learn to give Me your problems as they come to you.
Do not let them pile up all at once, until you are not able to think clearly.
I am you burden bearer.
Take courage and know that I AM in control of all things.
Put your trust in Me and you will be able to see that you can put your whole life into My Hands and trust that all things will come into order.
You will be able to live out your life and begin to enjoy it.
This is what I want for you, to walk in My Love, Joy, and Peace.
Go about your day and know you are blessed!

Matthew 11:28
Come unto me, all ye that labour and are heavy laden, and I will give you rest.

DAILY ENCOURAGING WORDS...*TO LIVE BY*

February 11th

Arise and shine for the Glory Light of Jesus has come!
Do you not know that I AM is in everyday, for I have made them from the beginning.
They were written down in My book from the beginning of time.
Your life has been written down in My book also from the beginning, even before you were born.
Everyday of your life has been planned from the beginning, to walk out those plans, you need to trust in Me, so you can achieve the plans I have planned for you.
In each day I will guide you and give you strength.
You cannot walk out your day in your own strength.
The enemy of your soul will try to take away all good things in your life. You are powerless against him.
I am the strength in you to overcome the enemy of your soul.
How you defeat him is to praise Me and keep your eyes on Me. Give him no open door to come into your life.
As you are a child of Mine, he has no power over you, unless you hive him that power. I stripped him at the Cross.

John 10:10

The thief cometh not, but for to steal, and to kill, and to destroy; I AM come that they might have life and that they might have it more abundantly.

365 Day Devotional...God still speaks today...John 10:27

DAILY ENCOURAGING WORDS...*TO LIVE BY*

February 12th

Arise and shine for the Glory Light of Jesus has come!
My hand is outstretched to you, My child.
Come and see what I have for you.
Release your faith and partake of all that I have for you.
Every part of your life is in My hands.
I am not a God that toys with your life.
My Word is truth and I watch over My Word to have it come to pass.
What I have spoken over your life will come to past as you put your faith and trust in Me.
I cannot lie and I AM faithful and true.
So, lift your voice and sing praises unto Me.
Expect and believe what I have said will come to past.
I love you My child and I will never leave you nor forsake you.

John 17.17
Sanctify them through thy truth; thy Word is truth.

DAILY ENCOURAGING WORDS...*TO LIVE BY*

February 13th

Arise and shine for the Glory Light of Jesus has come!

Press into Me, give Me all your concerns for this day.

As you give them to Me, you are letting go of the great weight that cause you to feel weary and seems hard for you to walk with Me.

My child be quick to learn that I AM is the ONE that can carry your burden, so that you can walk freely in Me.

You have a helper which is the Holy Spirit that resides in you.

When you are weary take the strength that comes from within you.

Walk with your head up high knowing that your God is working on your behalf.

Lean on Me and draw from Me.

Praise Me and honor Me and you will feel the strength of Me poor into you.

Give all to Me My child and walk with Me.

I love you; you are Blessed!

1st Peter 5:7

Casting all your care upon Him, for He careth for you.

DAILY ENCOURAGING WORDS...*TO LIVE BY*

February 14th

Arise and shine for the Glory Light of Jesus has come!
Take this day and look within yourself and take notice where you are with Me.
Let My Holy Spirit show you what is going on in your inner life.
The inner life is the life that only I can see, and it is the way you interact with Me.
This life is to line up with Me.
This life is to line up with the way your outer life is portrayed.
It is important to have both inner and outer life to line up with My Word.
Walk in the Holy Spirit al all times, this is the only way you will be able to walk according to My will for you so you can walk out your destiny.
it is very important to keep track of what is going on in you and around you, for it may not only affect you but also the people that are watching your life.
The whole purpose is to walk in My Light to Glorify Me in all that you do.

Psalms 119:105
The Word is a lamp unto my feet and a light into my path.

DAILY ENCOURAGING WORDS...*TO LIVE BY*

February 15th

Arise and shine for the Glory Light of Jesus has come!
Do you not know My child, that the only way to please Me
is to walk in righteousness and put your faith totally in Me.
When hard times come, be ready to look to Me for the
answer to solve whatever comes into your life.
There is nothing to great that I cannot handle and nothing
to small that I would overlook.
I have seen your heart and know your desires, for I was the
ONE who put those desires in your heart to begin with.
Open to Me and let Me transform you so that you will be
able to receive what I have for you.
If you are full of things that are not of Me, then those things
will stop Me from fulfilling what I want to do in you.
So, surrender all to Me and I will do the work in you so that
you are able to have the desires of your heart fulfilled.

Psalm 20:4
Grant thee according to thine own heart and fulfill all thy
counsel.

DAILY ENCOURAGING WORDS...*TO LIVE BY*

February 16th

Arise and shine for the Glory Light of Jesus has come!
Do you not see the Hand of your God move in your situation this day.
I AM faithful to My Word.
When things get out of hand and seem hopeless, that is when I love to move on behalf of My children.
Learn to keep your eyes on Me and not on the situation.
When you look at the situation, that it looks so big and there seems to be no way that you can do anything yourself, to take care of it.
You just get overwhelmed, and you have lost what hope that you had.
Just look up and come back to Me and put your faith in Me, for I AM waiting on you to trust Me to do the impossible for you.
That is what I want to do for all My children, if they would only let Me.

Matthew 19:26
But Jesus beholds them, and said unto them, with men this is impossible, but with God, all things are possible.

365 Day Devotional...God still speaks today...John 10:27

DAILY ENCOURAGING WORDS...*TO LIVE BY*

February 17

Arise and shine for the Glory Light of Jesus has come!
Walk with Me, My child, walk in the Light of My Glory.
My Glory will show you the way to walk when hard things come your way.
You will be able to walk through them for you are already walking in My Light.
My light will show you what to do to overcome the things that would seem to overtake you.
Everything you need is in Me, I AM the Light of the world.
I AM the truth and the way.
My way, there is no darkness.
My Light shines brightly before you.
You need not look elsewhere, for I AM in you.
So, look deep inside for all that you need.
Your strength cometh from Me.
I AM always with you, to guide you and teach you to keep you on the straight and narrow path.
Just follow Me.

John 8:12

Then spoke Jesus again unto them saying, I AM the Light of the world.
He that followth Me shall not walk in darkness but shall have the Light of Life.

365 Day Devotional...God still speaks today...John 10:27

DAILY ENCOURAGING WORDS...*TO LIVE BY*

February 18th

Arise and shine for the Glory Light of Jesus has come.
Take My Hand and know that all is well in My Hands.
I will lead you and show you the way that I want to take you.
Put your full trust in Me and do not doubt.
Let go of your own ideas of how you should walk out your faith in Me and allow Me to work in your life, every part of your life.
You will see that you will grow in all ways and become what I have call you for.
It is a matter of letting go of everything that you wanted and dreamed about, that does not line up with My Word.
I have called you to walk in My Light so you must let go of the darkness that would not allow you to walk with Me.
It is a matter of choice from your heart.
Make up your mind to do My will and not your own, and stand steadfast, do not waiver and allow Me to change you.
Press into Me and give Me praise with all your heart.

Romans 12:12
And be not conformed to this world but be ye transformed by the renewing of your mind, that ye may prove what that is good and acceptable, and perfect will of God.

365 Day Devotional...God still speaks today...John 10:27

DAILY ENCOURAGING WORDS...*TO LIVE BY*

February 19th

Arise and shine for the Glory Light of Jesus has come!
Let go the things that hold you back from My Hand being open to you.
Trust Me for all your needs and wants.
Does not My Word say that My God shall supply all your needs according to His riches in Glory by Christ Jesus:
Leave the fear behind and walk in faith.
Fear will tie My Hands so that I can do nothing for you.
But faith is the key that opens My Hand to Bless you.
My desire is to Bless you beyond what you can imagine.
Ask and see what I will do for you.
I long to Bless My children.
I have so much for you, think big and ask big.
You cannot think small and expect big.
Get rid of small thinking and reach higher.
That is what I want for you.
My children live way below what they could have, because of fear and unbelief.
I want to Bless them beyond what they could comprehend.
Step out in faith and ask big and believe.

Mark 11:24

Therefore, I say unto you, what thing soever ye desire, when ye pray, believe that ye receive them, and ye shall have them.

DAILY ENCOURAGING WORDS...*TO LIVE BY*

February 20th

Arise and shine for the Glory Light of Jesus has come!
Know in this day My Hand will move in your situation.
Do not be dismayed for I AM with thee.
Wherever you go I AM with you.
Get your eyes off things that are going on around you.
Put your eyes on Me, for I AM more powerful than anything that would come against you.
Put your faith in Me and rejoice in your SAVOUR.
Take up your cross and follow Me.
Leave everything behind and know that you are following the ONE that is in control of your life.
No need to be fearful for My Love, Joy, and Peace are within you.
Choose the things that are of Me and walk with Me.
Live in the now and never look back.
I AM a God that is always moving forward and that is what I want you to do.
You are Mine and I AM yours, put your hand in Mine and never let go, trusting Me all the way.

John 15:12

I AM the Vine; you are the branches. If you remain in Me and I in you, you will bear much fruit, apart from Me you can do nothing.

February 21st

Arise and shine for the Glory Light of Jesus has come!
When you are weary, look to Me.
Does My Word not say …let the weak say I AM strong?
when you speak forth My Word, there is the power to cause it to come to life.
Do not just read My Word but cause it to go deep into your spirit, so that when you need help the Holy Spirit will bring forth the very Word you need at that time.
Do not be just a reader of My Word but be doers of My Word also.
Stand steadfast on My Word and never give up.
In My Word, there is an answer for everything in your life.
Continue to put your life in My Hands and walk in faith to release all that is needed for a sound and joyful life.

Psalms 119:105
The Word is a Lamp unto my feet and a light unto my path.

February 22nd

Arise and shine for the Glory Light of Jesus has come?
Do you not know that I AM faithful that I keep My Word?
I watch over My Word, and it will not return unto Me void.
If I did not keep My Word, I would not be who I AM.
Everything that I created was by My Word.
If you believe in My written Word and put it deep in your heart; it will establish forth in, you and you will not find it hard to believe to stand on My Word for the answer to your prayers.
By faith My Word and My Power together will bring forth the answer to your prayers according to My will.
I can not go beyond My Word.
All things pass away, but My Word stands forever.
The Word is My will; that is why you need to stand on My Word in time of need.
Keep standing on My word and give thanks for the answer.
I do hear and answer the prayers of My children.

Matthew 1.1
But he answered and said, it is written, Man shall not live by bread alone, but by every word that proceedeth out of the mouth of God.

February 23rd

Arise and shine for the Glory Light of Jesus has come!
Come, I say come unto Me.
My arms are open to you this day, My eyes are upon you.
I see you and My ears are open to you.
I wait patiently for you to come and sit with Me, so that you can talk to Me and surrender all your hurt, all your needs and your wants. Give them all to Me.
You are My child, and I will exchange all the hurts, and give you all that I died to give you, so that you would be able to live life pleasing to Me.
That you walk in My strength, My Love, Peace, and Joy.
You will learn to walk in the Spirit and not in the natural side of life.
You are a Spiritual being first; you have a soul, and you live in a natural body.
I AM calling you to walk your life out in your Spirit man which relates to My Holy Spirit that resides within you, He is the one that gives you guidance in your life.
Rely on Him for all the help you need.

1st Corinthians: 11

For what man knoweth the things of a man, save the spirit of man which is in him? even so the things of God knoweth no man, but the Spirit of God.

DAILY ENCOURAGING WORDS...*TO LIVE BY*

February 24th

Arise and shine for the Glory Light of Jesus has come.
Have I not said that you are in the Palm of My Hand?
Have I not said that I would never leave you nor forsake you?
I AM a God that cannot lie, for only truth come from Me.
So, I know what you go through every minute of your day.
You can trust Me when things get out of hand and come to Me for direction.
I will show you what to do, so all will work out to benefit you and Glorify Me. All things work together for good to those that love Me.
You are called for My purpose.
I have already put My purpose in you, and I watch over you to guide you in the way you should go.
Don't try to do things your own way.
That will only bring hardship to you.
Trust and lean heavily on Me.
I AM always there for you.

Psalm 34:19
Many are the afflictions of the righteous; but the Lord delivered him out of them all.

365 Day Devotional...God still speaks today...John 10:27

DAILY ENCOURAGING WORDS...*TO LIVE BY*

February 25th
Arise and shine for the Glory Light of Jesus has come!
Come before Me with thanksgiving and praise on your lips and in your heart.
This is what I long for.
I see and hear My children praising Me from their hearts, knowing that I will respond to their praises.
I am a God of the heart.
Give Me your heart and see what I will do in your life.
There is nothing that I cannot do for I AM the God of the impossible.
There is nothing too great or too small for Me.
Surrender all to Me.
Faith in believing and I will work in you to cleanse you and make you whole.
Trust Me for I will cause your life to be a Blessing to Me and a Blessing to all that are around you.
I want to use you to be a mighty testimony for Me.
To let people see Me in you and for them to want what you have; for they will see the love joy and peace operating in your life.
Luke 18:27
...and he said, the things which are impossible with men are possible with God.

365 Day Devotional...God still speaks today...John 10:27

DAILY ENCOURAGING WORDS...*TO LIVE BY*

February 26th

Arise and shine for the Glory Light of Jesus has come!
Walk in the goodness of your God this day!
Be open to receive what I have for you today.
Also, be sure to keep yourself in a position with My Holy Spirit, so that you will be able to hear what He has to say this day.
Let nothing block out His voice; He is the source of your strength for everything you need is coming from Him.
He shows you what direction to take in your life and He also teaches you all truth and how to walk out your life before Me.
The very life of Me, flows out from the Holy Spirit to you.
Ask of Him, and He will give you the answer that you need.
Rely on Him and He will lead you and show you the answers to lead you out of any situation.
Trust and obey and you will never be disappointed.
He is always with you, and He will never leave you.
Go about your day and know that you are Blessed!

Psalm 34:8
O taste and see that the Lord is good, Blessed is the man that trusteth in Him.

365 Day Devotional...God still speaks today...John 10:27

DAILY ENCOURAGING WORDS...*TO LIVE BY*

February 27th

Arise and shine for the Glory Light of Jesus has come!
To walk in My Peace is the most Blessed gift to have.
It is the way that I want My children to walk in everyday of your lives.
When you are in peace with yourself and peace with everyone around you, that is when My Glory Light really shines and the Power flows without distractions and changes begin to happen around you.
The situations that you find yourself in are being dealt with and it wasn't hard at all.
My ways are not hard to do, if you only concentrate on Me and stay in My Word, to walk it out and always allow My Peace as the empire of your life.
If you don't have peace about doing something, do not do it.
Always take the time to spend in My presence and keep filled up with My Peace everyday.

Colossians 3:15
And let the peace of God rule in your hearts, to the which also ye are called in one body and be ye thankful.

DAILY ENCOURAGING WORDS...*TO LIVE BY*

February 28/29th

Arise and shine for the Glory Light of Jesus has come!
This day is a day of new beginnings.
My Mercies and Grace are new everyday.
Take hold of them and walk into the newness of this day.
As you come before Me and spend time before Me, I will fill you up and give you Strength and Power for this day.
Do not live in the past nor look to the future for I AM a now God and I work in the now.
There is only Strength and Power for this day.
This is an awesome day for I have made it.
Learn to walk in My ways and you will be fulfilled.
When you are of Me then life's troubles will seam very small in your sight; for I AM the power to cause your troubles to be worked out for your sake.
Keep looking to Me and put your rust in Me.
There is no other way; for I am the way, truth, and the Light.

Lamentations 3:22-23

22) It is of the Lord's mercies that we are not consumed, because His compassion fail not.

23) They are new every morning, great is thy faithfulness.

365 Day Devotional...God still speaks today...John 10:27

DAILY ENCOURAGING WORDS...*TO LIVE BY*

MARCH

Psalm 104:10

He sendeth the springs into the valleys, which run among the hills.

DAILY ENCOURAGING WORDS...*TO LIVE BY*

March 1st

Arise and shine for the Glory Light of Jesus has come!
Expect great things to happen this day.
As you go about your day, sing praises to Me, and let your heart rise in great expectations of what your God can do for you.
As you keep your eyes on Me and not on things around you, you will soar in the Glory and the Love that I have for you.
My Strength and Power will keep you going, and My Peace will be your guide.
When you walk in a state like this, there is nothing that can stop you from living in victory.
When you get to that place in your life, the people you are in contact with, will surely see Me living in you and the Power that is in you will draw them to Me.
They will give themselves to Me and come into My Kingdom.
The goal is to bring souls into My Kingdom.
Walk in Me this day...and be Blessed!

Philippians 4:7
And the peace of God, which passeth all understanding shall keep your heart and mind through Christ Jesus.

March 2nd

Arise and shine for the Glory Light of Jesus has come!
Press into Me this day and let Me flow in you and through you.
Let Me do a work within your spirit that will bring you higher and higher, far above all your problems of life.
You are seated in Heavenly places with Me.
When you have your eyes on Me, the problems of life seem so small.
I am able to help you with them and bring you through as long as you look to Me.
They are nothing in My Hands.
There is nothing impossible with Me.
Put your faith in Me and watch what I will do on your behalf.
You are blessed!

Ephesians 2:6
...And hath raised us up together in Heavenly places in Christ Jesus.

DAILY ENCOURAGING WORDS...*TO LIVE BY*

March 3rd

Arise and shine for the Glory Light of Jesus has come!
Let Me show you the way that you should go.
When you are weary, it is hard to see and think straight.
That is when you need to remember that you are not alone,
but you have the help that you need who lives inside of you.
Depend on the Holy Spirit to lead you and fill you up with His Strength,
You need never to think that you travel along this path of life alone.
Reach out to the ONE that knows the way and walk hand in hand with Him.
Look inside of yourself and there you will become strong again and you will be able to face the cares of this life.
You will know that all is well, for you know and trust the ONE within you.
All is well in His Hands.

Isaiah 40:29
He giveth power to the faint and to them that have no might.
He increaseth strength.

DAILY ENCOURAGING WORDS...*TO LIVE BY*

March 4th

Arise and shine for the Glory Light of Jesus has come!
Let it flow, let it flow!
Allow My Spirit (the Holy Spirit) to have full rein in your life.
There is no other spirit that has the power that lives in you.
He has the answer for all that may come against you in your life.
He is your Comforter, Helper, your Guide.
Do not grieve the Holy Spirit, for He is the ONE that gives you Strength, Wisdom, Joy, Peace, and the Love of God that is shed abroad in your heart.
Spend time with Him, give Him your full attention, so that He can fill you up each day.
You will then be equipped for your day; you will see how your day will pass without the tension of everyday stress.
So, you see the importance of spending time everyday with Him, is so important.
He is the Power to live by!

Ephesians 4:30
And grieve not the Holy Spirit of God, whereby ye are sealed unto the day of redemption.

DAILY ENCOURAGING WORDS...*TO LIVE BY*

March 5th

Arise and shine for the Glory Light of Jesus has come!
Do not go before Me, for I have already designed what you are to do in your walk with Me.
Notice I said, "with Me".
We are to walk hand in hand so that it will be done according to My Word.
I have already put in place what you will need to accomplish My will for you.
All you must do is be obedient and walk in it.
Be one with Me and My Holy Spirit which lives in you.
Listen closely to Him and do what He has to say, and you will not stray from your pathway of life.
You will be able to walk in Joy and Peace and it will not be burdensome.
My will for you is to enjoy your life and be a vessel of love to all that is around you.
Reach out to others and be a blessing to them.
Remember I AM always with you.

Luke 11:28
But He said, yea rather, blessed are they that hear the Word of God and keep it.

DAILY ENCOURAGING WORDS...*TO LIVE BY*

March 6th

Arise and shine for the Glory Light of Jesus has come!

I AM calling to the hearts of My children to return unto Me.

To put away the things of this world that has them in a state of bondage, to lay aside things that will carry them from off the true path that leads to Me.

Call out to Me and I will put you on the way that leads to Me.

My Love is strong toward you, and I will bring you through to lift you up to a higher place in Me.

There is no other way.

Keep calling out to Me and I will show you all that you need to do to walk in My ways.

It is all about Me, surrender all to Me.

I AM your guide and your strength.

Lean not unto your own understanding but lean on Me and trust Me that I will do as I have said.

Provers 3:6
In all thy ways acknowledge Him, and He shall direct thy path.

365 Day Devotional...God still speaks today...John 10:27

DAILY ENCOURAGING WORDS...*TO LIVE BY*

March 7th

Arise and shine for the Glory Light of Jesus has come!
It is a new day!
This is the day that the Lord has made, follow Me.
Look to e and inquire of Me the things that are on your mind.
There is nothing that I cannot do for you.
You need not try to work out things by yourself.
I AM just waiting on you to ask and believe in Me to answer you and give you direction in every situation that has come into your life.
I know everything about you, I made you and I long to give you a good life and see you overcome all that would come against you.
Lean on Me and praise Me and trust Me.
I AM your Strength.
Rely on Me for I AM there for you!

Psalm 16.1
God is our refuge and strength, a very present help in trouble.

DAILY ENCOURAGING WORDS...*TO LIVE BY*

March 8th

Arise and shine for the Glory Light of Jesus has come!

Praise Me, Praise Me.

Come to Me in thanksgiving and praise.

Honor Me for this is what gives Me great pleasure.

When you do this, it shows Me that you do not have your heart and mind on just you and what you want.

Yes, you need to put forth your request before Me, but do this in faith, believing that I hear and answer your prayers.

I long to hear your praises come up to Me that moves My hand on your behalf.

For I see a heart that is open to Me, that not only believes in Me but puts Me first in your life.

Your praises also break through and destroys the plans of the enemy (Satan).

He does not know what to do with this.

It is a Mighty tool to pull down the works of Satan.

So, My child continue walking in praises and worship unto your God.

Psalm 100:4

Enter into His gates with thanksgiving, and into His courts with praise, be thankful unto Him and bless His name.

365 Day Devotional...God still speaks today...John 10:27

March 9th

Arise and shine for the Glory Light of Jesus has come!
Wait on Me, do not go before Me.
Always keep your mind on Me and your eyes on Me.
That is the safe zone for you.
If you do this, you will not have a problem that you cannot handle for you are waiting on Me to show you how to handle it.
You will not be full of fear, but peace will fill your heart and your mind will be open to what I have for you.
You will always have situations arise in your life.
This situation that comes your way will cause you to grow spiritually if you do not allow the situation to rule you.
You take the authority over it.
In My name, there is the Power to solve that situation.
Always praise Me and trust Me to do what I have said.
My Word will come to pass.

Psalm 9:10
And they that put their trust in Thee, for Thou Lord hast not forsaken them that seek thee.

DAILY ENCOURAGING WORDS...*TO LIVE BY*

March 10th

Arise and shine for the Glory Light of Jesus has come!
Do you not know that the God of the whole world is looking down upon you and knows everything about you?
I created you for a higher calling than living day to day.
I have called you out of darkness into My Glorious Light.
In My Light is everything that life needs for you to have to live in the calling I have for you.
I have called you to love one another and to reach out beyond yourself and touch with My Love, those that are around you and everywhere you go.
I AM coming for a Bride without spot and without wrinkle that is why you must come up higher in Me.
Give Me all that keeps you from going higher in Me.
I will do the work in you that needs to be done.
I love you and you are ever so precious to Me.

John 15:12
This is My commandment, that ye love one another as I have loved you.

DAILY ENCOURAGING WORDS...*TO LIVE BY*

March 11th

Arise and shine for the Glory Light of Jesus has come!
Be still in your heart and in your mind, so that I can commune with you.
When your mind is busy and you think that you can figure out what is going on in all that confusion, there is no way out.
So, I say My child, let it all go and begin to release all that is on your mind, and surrender all to Me, so that I can give you instructions of what you should do.
Always consult Me first and in doing so, you will not have to go through the torment of the mind.
When your mind is clear, you will find that there will be My Peace operating in you.
When there is My Peace, there is joy in living your life for Me.
I will lead and guide you in the way that you should go.

Romans 8:6
For to be carnally minded is death; but to be spiritually minded is life and peace.

DAILY ENCOURAGING WORDS...*TO LIVE BY*

March 12th

Arise and shine for the Glory Light of Jesus has come!
Say nothing is too hard for My God.
I AM always waiting and listening for your prayers.
It does not matter what you pray for but believe that I heard and answer your prayers.
Ask anything in My name and I will do it for you.
Just believe and receive it.
Take it by faith and you shall have it.
All that is done of Me is done by faith.
Your walk is a walk of faith in Me, to do your destiny and your destination.
Lean on Me and trust Me to show you what you must do, and I have already put into place all that you will need.
Trust My Holy Spirit to help you and guide you all the way through.
You are never alone, so you need not fear.
Keep looing to Me and all will be well with you.

1st John 5:15

And if we know that He hears us, whatsoever we ask, we know that we have the petitions that we desired of Him.

DAILY ENCOURAGING WORDS...*TO LIVE BY*

March 13th

Arise and shine for the Glory Light of Jesus has come!
All good things come down from the Father above.
When you know and receive the Love of the Father, you know that His Love is unconditional.
You do not work for it but only receive it.
He longs for you to receive it and walk in it every day of your life.
You can face anything and accomplish whatever comes your way for you know that the Father loves you and is there to bring you through.
His love is already in you for the Holy Spirit sheds His Love abroad in your heart.
Let His Love work in you to bring forth His Joy and Peace and all the Gifts of the Spirit to grow and operate in your life.
You walk in Faith and Love; this is the key to walk out your destiny in Joy and Peace.

Romans 5:5
And hope maketh not ashamed; because the Love of God is shed abroad in our hearts by the Holy Spirit which is given to us.

365 Day Devotional...God still speaks today...John 10:27

DAILY ENCOURAGING WORDS...*TO LIVE BY*

March 14th

Arise and shine for the Glory Light of Jesus is come!

Fear not, for I AM with thee.

Wherever you go and whatever you do, I AM there for you.

Let Me show you what I can do in your day.

Lean not upon your own understanding for you will not be able to get the full picture of what you need to see, to accomplish what you want done.

Put aside all that you think and ask Me to orchestrate what you would like to be done.

When you walk in the Spirit and not in the flesh, you will see awesome things happen on your behalf.

I long to do many things for you, if only you would allow Me to work in you, so that you would be able to receive what is needed.

Just surrender all your life to Me and see what I will do for you.

Proverbs 3:5

Trust in the Lord with all thine heart and lean not unto thine own understanding.

DAILY ENCOURAGING WORDS...*TO LIVE BY*

March 15

Arise and shine for the Glory Light of Jesus has come!
Come to me child and sit at My feet.
Let go of everything that would lead you astray.
The darkness of this world is rising.
It has become gross darkness.
My Glory Light is also rising to cover the whole earth.
The darkness will not overtake the Glory Light, for greater is My Glory Light than the darkness of Satan.
There are only two Kingdoms.
There is the Kingdom of Satan, which is darkness, and the Kingdom f Light which is My Kingdom.
Those that walk in Me are well able to overcome the darkness because Greater is He that is in you, than he that is in the world.
So, take time and learn more and more of Me, so that you will be strong and walk out everything that My Word teaches you.
Now is not the time to be slack, but to be open to Me and filling yourself with My Word.
My Word is powerful in every situation that you may find yourself in. Speak My Word Forth...I will answer you.

Psalm 119:105

Thy word is a lamp unto my feet, and a light unto my path.

365 Day Devotional...God still speaks today...John 10:27

March 16th

Arise and shine for the Glory Light of Jesus has come!
Have you not heard that My Word is the guideline for your life.
Take My Word and put it before your eyes and read it so that My Word will overtake you and change you into the person that I have pre-ordained you to be, even before the foundation of the world.
As you put time aside for My Word, you will see the changes take place in you.
Do not be just hearers only but be doers of My Word.
Put My Word into practise and stand on My Word for it will never fail you.
Let it build you up in faith, as you partake of it daily.
It will renew you and make you strong and you will experience the Joy and Peace that will flood your spirit and mind.
My Word is the food for your spirit to become strong, just as you eat food in the natural to make your body strong.
As you eat daily of My Word you will become strong and healthy both in the Spirit and the body.

Proverbs 4:20, 21

My son, attend to My Words, incline thine ear into My sayings. Let them not depart from thine eyes; keep them in the midst of thine heart.

March 17th

Arise and shine for the Glory Light of Jesus has come!
Come and walk with Me this day.
Let My Glory Light shine through you this day.
I long to walk with my children day in and day out.
There is freedom in My Light.
You can see what all around you is, when you walk in My Light, for the darkness of this world is swallowed up by My Light.
It is a place of My Love, Joy, and Peace.
You can see clearly and have My Spirit to lead you and help you to decipher which is good or bad thoughts going through your mind.
Choose wisely, for your thoughts will determine which way you will walk.
The mind is a battle ground and Satan wants to rule it.
You are the one that has the power to take down every dark thought that tries to take over.
Be aware this day and walk in My Glory Light.

Philippians 2:5
Let this mind be in you, which was also in Christ Jesus.

DAILY ENCOURAGING WORDS...*TO LIVE BY*

March 18th

Arise and shine for the Glory Light of Jesus has come!
Let your mind not wander, that only gives Satan an opportunity to pull you off course.
Always keep your mind focussed, so that you will be able to accomplish what is at hand.
Never let your mind to negative ways.
That only lets the enemy (Satan) in so that you will not be able to focus on the things of the Spirit.
Put a guard upon your mind so that you will be focused on the things that pertain to Me.
When your mind is healthy, you will be happy, and you will be able to fulfill the task before you.
This will keep you stress free.
When you walk in Me and center your mind on Me, there is nothing that you will not be able to do.
Always keep your eyes on Me, for I AM your Stabilizer.

Isaiah 26:3
Thou wilt keep (him) in perfect peace (whose) mind (is) stayed (on Me); because he trusted in Thee.

DAILY ENCOURAGING WORDS...*TO LIVE BY*

March 19th

Arise and shine for the Glory Light of Jesus is come!
Look beyond your circumstances and see that I AM the answer to what you are facing.
You cannot see what I see for I know all things.
I see into the future, and I see what is going on in your life at the present time, for I AM an all-knowing God.
Allow yourself to be put into My Hands and expect Me to move on your behalf.
If you will do this, then you will allow Me to work on the situation at hand.
I will begin to move barriers out of your way, and you will be able to see and move closer to the answer that you need to solve your problem.
Do not fret!
Just keep your eyes on Me and put your trust in Me.
Just remember that I will never leave you nor forsake you.

Psalm 143:8
Cause me to hear thy lovingkindness in the morning; for in Thee do I trust.
Cause me to know that way wherein I should walk, for I lift up my soul unto thee.

365 Day Devotional...God still speaks today...John 10:27

DAILY ENCOURAGING WORDS...*TO LIVE BY*

March 20th

Arise and shine for the Glory Light of Jesus has come!
Come and go with Me.
Take My Hand and I will walk with you.
There are many things that I want to show you.
I want to take you higher in Me.
The higher you allow Me to take you, the higher above your circumstances, you will be able to see what is to be done.
When you are in Me, nothing is too hard to handle, for I AM all knowing and all seeing.
So, come higher and higher in Me.
All things can be accomplished in Me if your eyes and mind are stayed upon Me. It is possible to do that very thing.
Discipline yourself in My Word and put it deep into your spirit.
Every problem that arises, the answer is in My written Word.
Saturate yourself with it and you will see how powerful it really is.
It will work for you if you rely on it.

Proverbs 4:20
My son, attend to My word, incline thine ear unto my sayings.

DAILY ENCOURAGING WORDS...*TO LIVE BY*

March 21st

Arise and shine for the Glory Light of Jesus has come.

Let Me take you by your hand and show you what I have done for you already.

The first thing was giving you, My Salvation.

You received it by faith in Me and what I did on the Cross at Calvary.

That is where your Spirit life begun.

It has been a journey of faith for you and still will be unto the day I take you home to be with Me.

In the meantime, you will walk out your life, following Me and allowing My Holy Spirit to work in you and with you to do which I have put within, to fulfill your destiny.

It is already there, just receive it by faith and know that all is well.

Everything is put in place for your future, it is just walking into it.

I have a wonderful future for you if only you take it by faith.

Leave all else behind you and strive to walk it out by faith.

You are blessed My child.

Romans 8:28

And we know that all things work together for good to them that love God, to them who are the called according to (His) purpose.

365 Day Devotional...God still speaks today...John 10:27

DAILY ENCOURAGING WORDS...*TO LIVE BY*

March 22nd

Arise and shine for the Glory Light of Jesus has come!

My sheep hear My voice, I AM constantly talking to My children.

If you are not listening for My voice, you will miss the still small voice that is constantly trying to get your attention.

There are so many interferences in this world, trying to get the attention of My children.

If you are not minding the things of your Spiritual walk, you will not be open to My voice.

You must be constantly putting My Word into your heart, so that there will be no room for anything to penetrate your mind to get it off track.

Speak My Word over and over until it is settled in your heart.

Firmly planted, it will never leave you.

My Word has all the power to take you through anything that you must go through.

Speak the Word, believe the Word and stand on the Word.

It will never leave you; everything is surrounded by My Word.

Matthew 24:35

Heaven and earth shall pass away, but My Word shall not pass away.

DAILY ENCOURAGING WORDS...*TO LIVE BY*

March 23rd

Arise and shine for the Glory Light of Jesus has come!
Sit and be still in your thoughts.
The mind is a powerful thing.
That is where all things are decided.
It is very important to pay attention to what is going on in your mind.
The mind can contain a lot of different thoughts at one time.
It is important to decipher what is going in in your mind, this is where you need the Holy Spirit that lives within you to help you discern what is good or bad.
The enemy of your soul works in your mind to deceive you and pull you off track.
It is so important to get a hold of what goes on in your mind.
Satan comes for to steal, kill and destroy the good things that I AM doing in your life.
Be diligent and cast down all bad thoughts and clear your mind of them.

1st Peter 5:8

Be sober, be vigilant; because your advisory the Devil, as a roaring lion, walketh about, seeking whom he may devour.

365 Day Devotional...God still speaks today...John 10:27

DAILY ENCOURAGING WORDS...*TO LIVE BY*

March 24th
Arise and shine for the Glory Light of Jesus has come!
Come and step into My Glory Light!
My Glory Light is My presence.
It is everything that I AM.
My Joy, Peace, and My Love is in My presence.
My Power and Strength is in My presence.
Everything that I have is for you, My children.
I live in you by My Holy Spirit
I AM is close to you as the breath you breathe.
Your life is from Me.
Take all that I have given you and walk freely into it.
You will be free to do the works that I have called you to do.
As you continue to walk in My Light daily, you will see the growth that will take place in you.
You cannot but change when you walk in My presence day in and day out.
Be in My presence at the dawn of day and at the end of day, giving Me praise and honor that is due to Me.
My desire for My children is to be changing all the time, from Glory to Glory.
Ephesians 5:8
For ye were sometimes darkness, but now light in the Lord, walk as children of light.

365 Day Devotional...God still speaks today...John 10:27

DAILY ENCOURAGING WORDS...*TO LIVE BY*

March 25th

Arise and shine for the Glory Light of Jesus has come!
As you look upon a plant and you see how that plant grows, it first put into soil, and it is watered and put in a place to receive sunlight.

As it sits and it sits, it begins to grow.

If it has the soil, water, and sunlight, it will grow to its full size.

Well, My child, it is the same way with you, I have planted you in My Kingdom, you have been washed with My Blood.

I have given you My written Word, so that you will read it and put it into your spirit.

The Word washes away all that is not of Me.

It makes you clean inside.

I have given you My Glory Light, which shines in you and through you.

You need My Blood, My Word, and My Glory Light working in you so that you will be able to grow to the fullness of Me.

I have given you all you need to become what I have destined you to be, it is up to you to do your part.

We will work together.

1st Corinthians 6:11

And such were some of you; but ye are washed, but ye are sanctified, but ye are justified in the name of the Lord Jesus, and by the Spirit of our God.

DAILY ENCOURAGING WORDS...*TO LIVE BY*

March 26th

Arise and shine for the Glory Light of Jesus has come!
This is the day of rejoicing, to open to your God, and realize that I AM always for you and not against you.
There is nothing that could make your God keep the very things that I died for, from Blessing you.
My Love for you is everlasting.
Do not let Satan take away your Blessing that I have given you.
He can attack your mind and try to stop the Hand of God from working in your life, you are the only one that can stop the thoughts that come through your mind.
Always be aware of this and stop it before it takes a hold of your mind and causes fear.
Fear opens all kinds of things to come into your life.
So, stop Satan before that can take place in you.
No one can do this but you, My child, so be alert at all times.
Keep your mind on Me, that way Satan has no place to bring you down.

James 4:7
Submit yourselves therefore to God.
Resist the devil, and he will flee from you.

March 27th

Arise and shine for the Glory Light of Jesus has come!
Do you not think that I AM all-powerful, Almighty, the One that created all things, the world and all that it is?
I even created you and put you here on this earth for a reason.
I have set you apart from the rest, to do a special task for Me and My Kingdom.
You have a part that is not like any other, you are special and unique.
I have called you and I AM wanting to do a work in you to bring you to a place where you will walk out your destiny.
I AM asking you to allow Me to do that work in you.
I need you to surrender all to Me.
I cannot cross your will, that is why I need your permission.
Just surrender you whole life to Me and watch what I will do.

Proverbs 23;26
My son, give Me thine heart and let thine eyes observe My ways.

DAILY ENCOURAGING WORDS...*TO LIVE BY*

March 28th

Arise and shine for the Glory Light of Jesus has come!
Prepare yourself, and the way to do that is to seek My face daily, and come before Me, putting all in My Hands.
I care for you, that is why I say cast your cares upon Me.
The burdens that you carry are to overwhelming for you.
Under the loads of stress that you carry will cause you to go off the path I have put you on.
Realize right away that you are not able to handle the stress that comes with dealing with the things that you face everyday.
Roll it over unto Me, I AM your burden bearer.
Learn to walk in My strength, for it will carry you through everything that may come your way.
Remember to come to Me and release all to Me.
I AM always there for you.

Psalm 55:22
Cast thy burden upon the Lord and He will sustain thee.
He shall never suffer the righteous to be moved.

DAILY ENCOURAGING WORDS...*TO LIVE BY*

March 29th

Arise and shine for the Glory Light of Jesus has come!
Stand steadfast in what you believe, for it is everything that pertains to life.
I AM the life giver.
Believe in Me and My written Word, for out of it flows My Life and everything that you need to fulfill every part of your life.
There is not other way, for I AM the Way, the Truth, and the Life.
Everything you need is in My Word, and it will never fail you.
Stand on My Word and believe what is said and you will become what I have placed within you when you were in your mother's womb.
Everything is put in place for you, even your future.
You need to walk it out day by day and walk in faith, knowing that I AM is with you.
Work with the Holy Spirit and you will see your life come together, you will be fulfilled in everyway.
Always move forward, never stand still.

1st Corinthians 16:13

Watch ye, stand fast in the faith, quit you like men, be strong.

DAILY ENCOURAGING WORDS...*TO LIVE BY*

March 30th

Arise and shine for the Glory Light of Jesus has come.
Bring to Me all that trouble you.
You are not alone, for I AM your helper.
I AM just waiting on you, to allow Me into your life in ever way.
There is no limit to what I can do for you.
Do not limit yourself for Me from doing what I want to do for you.
Surrender all to Me that keeps your faith from reaching Me.
There is so much more that I have for you, if only you would allow Me to do what needs to be done in your life.
It is all up to you, for it is your will and it is by your will that you make the choice to give all to Me.
It is your decision, only yours.
Be wise in what you choose as life and death is in the power of the tongue.

Isaiah 43;18
Remember ye not the former things, neither consider the things of old.

DAILY ENCOURAGING WORDS...*TO LIVE BY*

March 31st

Arise and shine for the Glory Light of Jesus has come!

Be still and know that I AM God!

Cleanse your mind of all thoughts that are not beneficial to your lifestyle and will keep you from Me.

All things start in your mind as you make decision on what goes through your mind.

That is why you need your thoughts to line up with My Word.

Spend time in My Word and learn of Me.

When thoughts come into your mind, that do not correspond with My Word, take action and release them.

If you do not do this right away, they have time to take root and begin to cause you trouble.

You have My Name and the Blood to come against wrong thoughts.

Release My Name, My Word, and My Blood and you will see how powerful they all are, do not let them be dormant.

Romans 12:2

And be not conformed to this world but be ye transformed by the renewing of your mind, that ye may prove what is good and acceptable, and perfect will of God.

DAILY ENCOURAGING WORDS...*TO LIVE BY*

APRIL

Song of Solomon 2:1

I am the rose of Sharon, and the lily of the valleys.

DAILY ENCOURAGING WORDS...*TO LIVE BY*

April 1st

Arise and shine for the Glory Light of Jesus has come!
Sit down at My feet; for I have things that I want to show you.
I need your attention, all of it, so I can talk to you without any distractions.
There are so many voices out there, that are trying to get My children's attention.
So, you must be in a place where you can get filled up with My Holy Spirit, which is at My feet.
That is why Mary chose to sit, at My feet.
She knew that she needed to listen and learn of Me.
There are many rewards in doing so.
You will find that there is joy and peace in My presence and in joy and peace, to overcome everyday living.
You need to be full of Me, which is walking in the Holy Spirit, day in, and day out.
It takes time and effort to sit at My feet, to be restored each day, not just once in awhile.

Luke 10:39
...and she had a sister called Mary, which also sat at Jesus' feet and heard His words.

DAILY ENCOURAGING WORDS...*TO LIVE BY*

April 2nd

Arise and shine for the Glory Light of Jesus has come!
Who are those that stand before the king:
They are those that are washed in the Blood of the Lamb that have surrendered their lives totally abandoned of themselves.
You become a soldier of the Cross, leaving all behind and going forward, living whole heartedly for your king.
There is no room for self and the world's ways.
Your life is full of the things of the Spirit, and not of the flesh.
Your eyes are totally locked upon your King, ready always to obey and go forth into the battle of life.
You totally rely on the strength that cometh from Him.
Never counting on yourself until the day you stand before the King of Kings and the Lord of Lords.
Look unto Him the Author and Finisher of your faith.

Revelation 9:16
...and He hath on His vesture and on His thigh a name written, King of Kings, and Lord of Lords.

365 Day Devotional...God still speaks today...John 10:27

DAILY ENCOURAGING WORDS...*TO LIVE BY*

April 3rd

Arise and shine for the Glory Light of Jesus has come!
Come and let us reason together.
I am waiting on you to come unto Me, so that you can reveal every thought and desire to Me.
I will show you what is on My Heart for you.
Be not afraid to tell Me what is on your mind.
I already know but it is important for you to tell Me, so that by doing so the down cast spirit it is released from your soul and the power it had over you has lost its hold on you.
I AM your Father and My LOVE for you is unconditional.
I only have good things for your life.
Learn to trust Me more and walk in MY ways.
You will see a great change in Your life.
Remember all good things come from My Hand, there is no mixture.

James 1:17
Every Good Gift and every Perfect Gift is from above, and comes down from the Father of Lights, with whom there is no variation or shadow in turning.

365 Day Devotional...God still speaks today...John 10:27

DAILY ENCOURAGING WORDS...*TO LIVE BY*

April 4th

Arise and shine for the Glory Light of Jesus has come.

There will be no greater time than right now, for you can live a full life in Me.

I have already prepared your life to the fullest.

It is written in My Book, one day at a time, of what you would be and everything that you need has already been put in place for you.

The way that it will come to past, is for you to set aside your will for the flesh and set your will and your mind on Me and the things of the Spirit.

It is day by day that you walk out My plans for you.

You have the Holy Spirit inside of you to help you, show you what to do for each day.

Ask and He will lead you.

Spend time with Him.

Nothing is more important than that.

Without the help of the Holy Spirit, you are stumbling and do not see clearly.

Let this day be the first day of the rest of your life and make the choice to walk with the Holy Spirit.

Psalm 32:8

I will instruct thee and teach thee in the way which thou shalt go.

I will guide thee with Mine eyes.

April 5th

Arise and shine for the Glory Light of Jesus has come!
Do you not see that all you have, has come from Me?
I AM always looking to give you good things and lead you in the way that you should go. The only way that I can lead you to the way you should go is if you are open and willing to let Me.
I need your will to work with Me so that there will be no hindrance in you to stop My Hand from working in your life.
My Hearts desire is to give you your hearts desire, for I have already put those desires in your heart.
Let us work together so that you will have the life that I died to give you.
Just receive and have a thankful heart toward Me, for what I have done for you and will continue to do so.

Psalm 37:4
Delight yourself in the Lord, and He will give you the desires of your heart.

DAILY ENCOURAGING WORDS...*TO LIVE BY*

April 6th

Arise and shine for the Glory Light of Jesus has come!
Rest in Me, My child, when you are weary.
Trust that I will restore you so that you will be able to undertake all that you have to do in your day.
Put Me first so that I can pour My Strength into you for your tasks at hand.
When you get weary in your body, then your mind becomes weary also, making it hard to deal with what is before you.
That is why I say to you, put Me first.
When you are filled up with Me and My strength is flowing in your body and your mind, it causes you to be able to make right choices in everything you do.
So, be alert and do your part and I will do My part.
We will work together to accomplish the goal that is before you.
Remember to put Me first in your day and put Me last at the end of your day.
All will go well with you, and your rest will be sweet.

Proverbs 8:17
I love them that love Me, and those that seek Me early shall find Me.

DAILY ENCOURAGING WORDS...*TO LIVE BY*

April 7th

Arise and shine for the Glory Light of Jesus has come!
Lift your head and look unto Me, the author and finisher of your faith.
As you put your faith in Me and begin to ask of Me, I will honor your request, for it is written, whatsoever you ask in My Name, I will do it.
Do not doubt in your heart and you will have it.
It is only when you allow fear to come in and steal what request you have already asked for that you will lack.
Fear is very subtle, it starts in your mind and if you do not recognize the thought and put it out of your mind, that thought will grow and you have then let the door open to Satan to come in and steal your faith and in turn stop your request from being manifested.
Keep a guard on your thoughts so that all will be well with you.

John 14:14
If you ask Me anything in My Name, I will do it.

DAILY ENCOURAGING WORDS...*TO LIVE BY*

April 8th

Arise and shine for the Glory Light of Jesus has come!
Set yourself aside from all things that have no value for your walk with Me.
These things will only take away the time that you would spend with Me.
In doing so, you become weak in your Christian walk.
Each day you need to put Me first and you need to keep your mind on the things that would keep you strong in Me.
That would be the written Word, for that is the only thing that has power to keep you strong.
Fill your mind with My Word, so that you will be able to walk in My Love and Joy and Peace.
In doing so you will be able to overcome anything that would come from hearing My Word, which is the power that you need.
My Word needs to be fresh everyday.
So, fill up on My Word and you will always be going forward in Me.

Luke 11:28
But He said, yea rather, Blessed are they that hear the Word of God and Keep it.

DAILY ENCOURAGING WORDS...*TO LIVE BY*

April 9th

Arise and shine for the Glory Light of Jesus has come!
Come unto Me, ye that are heavy laden, and I will give you rest.
Give me all that troubles you and watch what I will do for you.
I cannot do anything until you surrender all to Me.
Once you do this, I go to work on what you have given Me, and you will see the results of your troubles resolved.
You need not try to resolve them on your own, for you cannot see what I see and if you lean unto your own understanding it will only create more problems.
So, step out in faith, knowing that I do all things well.
Trust in Me always and never take your eyes off Me.

1st Peter 5:7

Casting all your care upon Him, for He careth for you.

DAILY ENCOURAGING WORDS...*TO LIVE BY*

April 10th

Arise and shine for the Glory Light of Jesus has come!
Do you not know that My Love is unconditional towards you?
My Son Jesus paid the price in full for your sins by shedding His Blood for you at Calvary.
All you must do is receive this gift and walk in it, every moment of your day.
When I look at you, I see My Son Jesus and everything that He has, you have.
You are co-heirs with Jesus.
I love you like I love My Son Jesus.
Reach out in faith and believe and take this love.
You are a new creature in Christ, old things are passed away and all things has become new.
So let go of the past and walk in the new.
This is a faith walk ad only by faith can you receive the new.

2nd Corinthians 5:17
Therefore, if any man be in Christ, he is a new creature: old things are passed away; behold, all things are become new.

DAILY ENCOURAGING WORDS...*TO LIVE BY*

April 11th

Arise and shine for the Glory Light of Jesus has come!
Let Me be your guide and your helper.
Be not worried about the things that could happen or should have happened.
You cannot see into the future, so why put your mind on it?
Do not allow your thoughts to wonder into the future, for I AM the one that knows what will happen in the future.
It is not for you to know for you would not be equipped for it, for you can only live in the present and the now.
So, do not let yourself miss what I have for you in this day and this hour.
Put your trust in Me, knowing that I already have been there, and all is well for you.
It is already prepared for you.
Your part is to stay close to Me and always looking to Me, your Author and Finisher of your faith.
So, continue to walk out your faith in Me and allow each day to become a blessing to you.

Deuteronomy 31:8
And the Lord, He it is that doth go before thee, He will be with you. He will not fail thee, neither forsake thee, fear not, neither be dismayed.

365 Day Devotional...God still speaks today...John 10:27

DAILY ENCOURAGING WORDS...*TO LIVE BY*

April 12th

Arise and shine for the Glory Light of Jesus has come!
I AM, the One who put the stars into space.
I AM, the one that created the earth and all that is within it.
I made it for mankind.
Everything that was made, I had mankind in mind, and I still do this day.
I look upon My children and I see their need for Me.
I AM here to meet all their needs, if only they would look to Me, the One that loves them so.
I AM the only one that can bring them through any situation that should arise in their lives.
They look upon the situation and all they see is how can I do this, how can I overcome this.
I say unto you, instead of looking at the situation, look unto Me and let your faith rise up and release it.
Know that whatever is going on in your life that seems so big and overbearing to you I AM your problem solver.
I can and I will work it out for you.
Just give it to Me and believe that it is done for you.

Psalm 34:6

This poor man cried, and the Lord heard (him) and saved him out of all his troubles.

DAILY ENCOURAGING WORDS...*TO LIVE BY*

April 13th

Arise and shine for the Glory Light of Jesus has come!
Come unto Me and I will give you rest.
I will lead you into the path of righteousness.
There you will find peace and a knowing that all is well in My Hand.
When your heart is right toward Me, there is no fear, no worry.
There is no fear, no worry in Me, for this is from the dark side and I AM full of light.
Light always produces peace and gentleness.
Love flows from Me for I AM Love.
You are of Me, so you also have My Love in you.
Let that love grow more and more in you each day.
Spend time in My Word and in My presence and it will cultivate My Love in you.
When you walk in My Love, then you are showing people around you that you are a child of mine.

1st John 4:8
He that loveth not knoweth not God, for God is Love.

365 Day Devotional...God still speaks today...John 10:27

DAILY ENCOURAGING WORDS...*TO LIVE BY*

April 14th

Arise and shine for the Glory Light of Jesus is come!
Trust in Me, I AM the one you can come to in your troubled hour. There is nothing that you cannot tell Me, for I know your thoughts even before you speak them out.
You need not be afraid to speak your mind.
Once you release your thoughts, the power that they had over you is gone.
The mind is powerful and if left unattended, it will cause you to do the very thing that you would not want to do.
So, be always on guard to know what thoughts are going through your mind.
That is how Satan gets in, is through your thoughts.
Ask for the gift of discernment to help you take control of your thought life and cast out the wrong thoughts and would cause you to stumble.
Remember you have the Holy Spirit within you to be your helper in time of need.

Isaiah 26:3
Thou wilt keep (him) in perfect peace, (whose) mind (is) stayed (on Thee) because he trusted in Thee.

365 Day Devotional...God still speaks today...John 10:27

DAILY ENCOURAGING WORDS...*TO LIVE BY*

April 15th

Arise and shine for the Glory Light of Jesus has come!
I AM the Alpha and Omega, the beginning, and the end.
There is no other God beside Me.
I AM your Father, you are made in My image.
You are mine and I AM yours.
You are in the Palm of My Hand.
My eyes are continually watching over you.
There are many trials and temptations that will come into your life, but these are sent to try you and to make you strong if you allow the Holy Spirit to work in you, to overcome these trials and temptations.
I was tried and tempted and so must you.
I overcame the world, and you can also for the power to overcome is within you when you keep your eyes on Me.
Trust in Me and daily, put your hand in Mine and I will never let go of you.
Never forget this, that is the truth and the life in Me.
All things flow from Me.

John 16:33

These things I have spoken unto you, that in Me ye might have peace, in the world ye shall have tribulations, but be of good cheer, I have overcome the world.

DAILY ENCOURAGING WORDS...*TO LIVE BY*

April 16th

Arise and shine for the Glory Light of Jesus has come!
Let the rays of My Glory Light surround you and let it penetrate your whole being.
This is My very Presence and Power in your life, to conquer your day.
As you walk in My ways and follow Me and put your faith and trust in Me, there will be no turning back. You will be so intrigued with Me, and you will have experienced the truth of the faithfulness of your God.
You will see that there is no darkness nor any evil thing in Me.
I AM full of Light and My Light will show you the way you should go.
My written Word will give you directions for your life.
You have all the power within you to become the overcomer that I see in you. Continue to walk daily in My ways and you will be fulfilling every part of your life.
I will sustain you in your walk with Me.

Philippians 4:13
I can do all things through Christ which strengthened me.

DAILY ENCOURAGING WORDS...*TO LIVE BY*

April 17th

Arise and shine for the Glory Light of Jesus has come.
Lift your head and walk with confidence that I AM your God.
Look to no other for I AM everything that you need to conquer the problems in your life, it doesn't matter big or small.
I AM interested in every part of your life, and I have the answer to all.
You can walk in the sureness, knowing that I AM always looking over you and that I see and know all things.
So, daily release to Me and expect Me to move on your behalf.
Walk in love and peace to release your faith in Me to do what needs to be done for you.
Each day you will grow in Me, and your faith will become stronger and stronger, always going ahead not staying still in one place.

Romans 8:37
Nay, in all these things, we are more than conquerors through Him that loved us.

DAILY ENCOURAGING WORDS...*TO LIVE BY*

April 18th

Arise and shine for the Glory Light of Jesus has come.

Great is Thy faithfulness, from morning to morning, Thy Mercies are new each day.

Yes, I AM faithful to My Word and My Mercy is to all that would allow Me to touch their lives.

I AM looking for My children to come and let Me Bless them and to open to Me to allow Me to work in every part of their lives, I AM wanting to make you whole.

When you are whole, then you will not be looking to anyone or anything to satisfy the longing that is in your heart.

The only One that can satisfy you is Me.

I AM your God and I put that longing in your heart, so therefore, I AM the only one that can make you fulfilled in every part of your life.

So, I say come to Me and I will do the work that needs to be done and you will walk out the rest of your life complete and fulfilled.

This is the way life is to be, that has been My way all along, to see My children made in My likeness, for you are made in My image.

Deuteronomy 7:9

Know therefore that the Lord thy God, the faithful God, which keeps covenant and mercy with them that love Him and keep His commandments to a thousand generations.

DAILY ENCOURAGING WORDS...*TO LIVE BY*

April 19th

Arise and shine for the Glory Light of Jesus has come!
From the beginning, I have known your pathway of life, for I was the One that put your life together.
I knew your thoughts and what you will say when you open your mouth.
It is My will for you to have a mind that will only bring forth life in every situation.
You have the power to stop any negative thoughts from coming out of your mouth.
You must choose the right thing and you do this by using discernment.
Ask the Holy Spirit to give you, His discernment.
You are not alone, the Holy Spirit lives in your spirit.
He is your helper.
Do not be slack in asking Him to help you in time of need.
Learn to walk together with Him.
When you do this, you will have peace, for you know He has all the right answers.

Job 22:21
Acquaint now thyself with Him, and be at peace, thereby good shall come unto thee.

DAILY ENCOURAGING WORDS...*TO LIVE BY*

April 20th

Arise and shine for the Glory Light of Jesus has come!
Wait on Me.
Take the time to sit quietly in My presence.
This is where you will find peace and you will learn of Me.
I will teach you how to open up to Me and I will tell you things you need to know about your life and what I expect for you.
We are partners one with the other.
We will work together to accomplish what I have already planned for your life.
I call upon you to trust Me and to walk with Me every day.
Keep your eyes on Me and your ears open to hear My voice.
You cannot know what will come your way, in your day, but I do see and know, and I AM able to steer you from any destruction coming your way.
So, be aware of what is going on around you, and be aware of what is going through your mind.
Get rid of all negative thoughts, if you don't, they will poison your life, do not allow this to happen.

Psalm 143:2

Cause me to hear thy lovingkindness in the morning, for in Thee do I trust. Cause me to know the way wherein I should walk, for I lift up my soul unto Thee.

365 Day Devotional...God still speaks today...John 10:27

DAILY ENCOURAGING WORDS...*TO LIVE BY*

April 21st

Arise and shine for the Glory Light of Jesus has come!
Take joy in knowing that our God is always watching over you.
So, learn to relax in My presence and know when your mind is clear from all the noise and thoughts coming and going through your mind.
You will be able to hear My voice clearer and then you will know what I AM saying to you.
It is very important that you spend time in my presence, to lift you above all the business of the world around you.
You live in this world, but you are not part of this world.
To be successful, you must live in a place that is in Me and trust that everyday will be successful because of it.
There is only one way and that is My way.
All you need is found in Me.
Learn to trust Me and do not falter, but follow Me.

1st John 2:15

Love not the world, neither the things (that are) in the world.
If any man loves the world, the love of the Father is not in him.

DAILY ENCOURAGING WORDS...*TO LIVE BY*

April 22nd

Arise and shine for the Glory Light of Jesus has come!
This is the time and hour to be fully aware of what is going on around you and in you.
Search your heart and let go of things that are not letting you go deeper in your God.
I AM calling for My people to walk in My purity and to walk in My light and power.
To do this, you must give Me all the things that cause you to become stagnant in Me and cannot go forward in My Kingdom.
I am looking for you to surrender all and be filled with My Holy Spirit and by keeping your eyes on Me, so there will be nothing that would keep you from going forward in Me.
Shut out the things of this world and commit all to Me.
You will walk in My power and strength.
Also, put your faith in Me and praise Me and walk in My Love.

John 8:2

Then spake Jesus again unto them, saying, I am the light of the world, he that followeth Me shall not walk in darkness but shall have the light of life.

DAILY ENCOURAGING WORDS...*TO LIVE BY*

April 23rd

Arise and shine for the Glory Light of Jesus has come!
Stand before Me and know that all is well for you have surrendered your life to Me.
You are washed in My Blood, and you stand in My Righteousness because of it.
There is nothing more that can be done.
I did it all for you on the cross when I rose from the dead, I took back all things that Satan had stolen from mankind.
I defeated him at the cross and made an open show of the principalities and power, triumphing over them.
You can walk in victory because of this.
If you open a door by stepping out of your protection under Me, you will be attacked by Satan.
You will have given him the power to do so.
The only way to get back in step with Me is to repent and turn back to Me.
My Blood will cover you and close the door that you opened.
Learn not to give Satan any open door to your life.
Walk in love and keep your mind clear of any negative thoughts.

1st Corinthians 6:14

...and God hath both raised up the Lord and will also raise us up by His power.

DAILY ENCOURAGING WORDS...*TO LIVE BY*

April 24th

Arise and shine for the Glory Light of Jesus has come!
Set aside all things that are blocking the Holy Spirit from getting through to you,
It not only keeps the Holy Spirit from leading you, but it also opens the door for Satan to work in you, to take away all the good things that I have given you.
Stay in the Word so that you will be grounded, and it builds your faith.
The Word and faith work together.
This takes time then you can determine when that will be.
Pull yourself away from all distractions and spend the time with Me, in My presence.
For in My presence is the Joy of the Lord, it is your strength.
You cannot depend on yourself, for your strength does not come from the natural realm.
You need to stay in the spiritual realm, for this is how you overcome.
Keep your eyes on Me and your hand in Mine.

Proverbs 30:5
Every word of God is pure. He is a shield unto them that put their trust in Him.

365 Day Devotional...God still speaks today...John 10:27

April 25th

Arise and shine for the Glory Light of Jesus has come!
Let us walk in the light, for in the light is everything that you need. As I AM the Light, so are you.
The Holy Spirit that lives within you is also light.
You are made in My image.
Darkness and Light cannot inhabit together.
You will live in the Light, or you will choose darkness.
To live a life that would totally satisfy, this is a life that is committed to Me.
There is no room for darkness, for darkness is like cancer, it will overtake you and your Light will surely become dim and ineffective.
Now is the time to make the choice.
Do not let anything keep you from committing totally to Me.
You know not the hour in which I will becoming for My Bride.
Make yourself ready and keep looking for Me to come as if it were today.

Deuteronomy 6:5
And thou shall love the Lord thy God with all thine heart, and with all thy soul and with all thy might.

DAILY ENCOURAGING WORDS...*TO LIVE BY*

April 26th

Arise and shine for the Glory Light of Jesus has come!
Rejoice, rejoice in Me this day, for I see all that is happening in your life.
Let not your heart be troubled, for your God goes before you, working on your behalf.
Never forget that I AM always with you.
I know your thoughts even before you think them.
I AM the All-knowing God.
Put Me at the helm of your life and trust Me.
I have nothing but good things for your life.
Put your hand into My Hand and never let go and do not look back.
Always be looking forward, for I want you to be always going forward, trusting Me, and praising Me for all things.
I love you with an everlasting Love.

Psalm 139:2
You know when I sit down and when I get up.
You know my thoughts before I think them.

365 Day Devotional...God still speaks today...John 10:27

DAILY ENCOURAGING WORDS...*TO LIVE BY*

April 27th

Arise and shine for the Glory Light of Jesus has come!
Come and spend your day with Me.
Sit at My feet and learn of Me.
I want to teach you many things that will benefit you, so that you will be able to take what I give you to work in your life.
It is important to spend time with Me and put My Word into you.
For your Spirit needs to be fed as it is what you must feed your spiritual body.
Your spirit grows when you spend time in My Word and in My presence.
I long to spend time with you.
I love you and you were created to fellowship with Me, for I put this within you.
This is why you never feel fulfilled within yourself.
You feel empty.
Come to Me and I will fill you up.
Put your trust in Me.

Matthew 4:4
But He answered and said, it is written, man shall not live by bread alone, but by every word that proceedeth out of the mouth of God.

365 Day Devotional...God still speaks today...John 10:27

DAILY ENCOURAGING WORDS...*TO LIVE BY*

April 28th

Arise and shine for the Glory Light of Jesus has come!
I stand at the door of your heart, and I knock, and I wait to see if you will open to Me.
I long for My children to ever be ready and willing for Me to come and fellowship with them.
That is the longing of My heart.
I long to spend time with you and show you how much I love you.
When you take time out of your busy life for Me, I will touch your life and bless you beyond what you could ever imagine.
If you don't spend time in My presence, I cannot minister to you, the way I want to.
Do not let the cares of this world keep you bound but rise above the things of this world and surrender your heart to Me and you will see change come over you.
If you do not allow Me to come into your life, you tie My Hands from working on your behalf.
Unlock the door of your heart and surrender to Me in all areas of your life.

Proverbs 23:26
My son, give Me thine heart, and let thine eyes observe My ways.

365 Day Devotional...God still speaks today...John 10:27

DAILY ENCOURAGING WORDS...*TO LIVE BY*

April 29th

Arise and shine for the Glory Light of Jesus has come!
Do not underestimate the power that is within you.
This power is the Power of your Almighty God.
This Power has the means to save you, to heal you, to cleanse you and make you whole in every part of your life.
Keep yourself connected with the Holy Spirit, and there is nothing that can stop you from all that your Father has for you.
If you pull away, you are the one that stops the Power of God working with you.
Remember that you have the choice.
I say choose life and live a victorious and fulfilled life.
Take each day and be thankful for all I have done and will do for you.
Just allow Me to continue working within your life, so that you become what I already put within you.
You and I will work together to achieve it.
I am always with you, and I love you very much.

Proverbs 3:6
In all thy ways acknowledge Him, and He shall direct thy path.

DAILY ENCOURAGING WORDS...*TO LIVE BY*

April 30th

Arise and shine for the Glory Light of Jesus has come.

Come unto Me and I will give you rest.

When you are weary and your mind seems to be overwhelmed and cannot work the way that I have created to work, stop, and surrender all to Me.

Learn to lean into Me and let Me take over and let My Holy Spirit settle your mind.

Learn to give Me your problems as they come to you.

Do not let them pile up all at once until you are not able to think straight.

I AM your Burden Bearer.

Take courage and know that I AM in control of all things.

Put your trust in Me and you will be able to see that you can put your whole life into My Hands to trust that all things will come into order.

You will be able to live out your life and begin to enjoy it.

This is what I want for you, to walk in My Love, My Joy, and My Peace.

Go about your day and know you are blessed.

Matthew 11:28

Come unto Me, all ye that labour and are heavy laden, and I will give you rest.

DAILY ENCOURAGING WORDS...*TO LIVE BY*

MAY

Song of Solomon 2:12

The flowers appear on the earth; the time of the singing of birds is come, and the voice of the turtle is heard in our land;

DAILY ENCOURAGING WORDS...*TO LIVE BY*

May 1st

Arise and shine for the Glory Light of Jesus has come!
Come unto Me, you who are weary, for I will give you rest.
Lay down your burdens and take on My rest, for you are not made to carry a load of life upon you.
It will bring you to such a place in your life that it will destroy you.
I have made a way for you to walk in the goodness of Me and I will take care of the load of burdens that you are carrying.
If you will only give them to Me.
As you give them to Me, you will feel the heaviness leave and I will give you My Strength to restore you to Me.
Be always open to Me, for I AM a God that wants to live in you and lead you to a place in your life that you will be able to touch other people's lives for Me.
That is My perfect will for your life.
Surrender completely to Me and you will be blessed.

Matthew 11:28
Come to Me, all you who are weary and burdened, and I will give you rest.

365 Day Devotional...God still speaks today...John 10:27

DAILY ENCOURAGING WORDS...*TO LIVE BY*

May 2nd

Arise and shine for the Glory Light of Jesus has come!
Walk in My footsteps, how you do this, is to study My Word and as you read and understand what it is saying to you.
Take that Word and put it into practice in your life.
My Word is like a mirror.
As you see what I did, then you can do the very same thing.
Become very aware of My life and how I lived out My life here on earth.
I relied on My Father and did only what He said, and I followed it out in My actions.
You have the Holy Spirit living inside of you.
Give ear to Him and as He leads you, you do as He says.
He is your Helper and your Guide, as My Father did for Me.
As I trusted My Father, so should you trust the Holy Spirit inside of you.

Luke 11:28
But He said, yea rather, blessed are they that hear the Word of God, and keep it.

DAILY ENCOURAGING WORDS...*TO LIVE BY*

May 3rd

Arise and shine for the Glory Light of Jesus has come!
Seek Me on all matters of life.
If you trust in Me, there is nothing that is too small or too hard for Me.
Do not try to think in your own mind or reason out the problems that you face.
The more you think about it, the bigger it gets in your mind.
When you do this, you allow Satan to cause fear and doubt to start to work within you.
Things start to close in on you and you cannot seem to see a way out, but I say unto you, be still and know that I AM God.
You are in the palm of My Hand, and I say give it all to Me for I have the answer to all problems, that would arise in your life.
It is a step of faith, so take that step of faith and turn your problems over to Me.
When you are still, then and only then can I lead you out of these problems.
I love you and will never leave you.
I AM is your answer for this day.
1st Peter 5:7
Casting all your care upon Him, for He careth for you.

365 Day Devotional...God still speaks today...John 10:27

DAILY ENCOURAGING WORDS...*TO LIVE BY*

May 4th

Arise and shine for the Glory Light of Jesus has come!
Surrender all your life to Me.
To grow in Me, as you surrender to Me and have faith that I will fully change you.
It means all not just what you want, you make a commitment to Me, so your life belongs to Me, and we will work together to get you ready to live the life I have laid out for you.
Give Me all your dreams if you trust Me, I was the one that planted those dreams in you, now you need to walk close to Me and learn of Me, through reading My Written Word and put it in your Spirit.
The Word heals the mind and soul.
Let My Holy Spirit teach you and lead you in the way you should go.
I AM coming for the ones that are looking for Me and the ones that are willing to let Me change them.
I want your life to be like a mirror of Me.
You are called to be Christ like, full of love, joy, and peace.
Without these attributes operating in your life, you are powerless.
Learn quickly to be obedient to Me.

Revelation 22:12

And behold, I come quickly, and My rewards is with Me, to give every man according as his work shall be.

365 Day Devotional...God still speaks today...John 10:27

DAILY ENCOURAGING WORDS...*TO LIVE BY*

May 5th

Arise and shine for the Glory Light of Jesus has come!
As the sun shines in a new day, so shines My Glory Light
upon you, not just one day but everyday.
So, look to Me and receive what I have for you.
If you ask in faith and believe in your heart, I long to give
what you ask to you.
Empty your mind and heart of anything that is not of Me
and begin to praise and honour Me and see how things will
change for you.
Without faith you cannot please Me.
Lean on Me and learn of Me.
This walk is the walk of FAITH.
When you received Me in Salvation, it was by faith.
When you received the gift of the Holy Spirit, you received
it by faith.
Everything you do in Me or for Me is done by faith.
You need not fear for I am with you.
Do not walk in fear but in faith.
Go about your day and walk by faith.

Hebrew 11:1
Now faith is the substance of things hoped for, the evidence
of things not seen.

DAILY ENCOURAGING WORDS...*TO LIVE BY*

May 6th

Arise and shine for the Glory Light of Jesus has come!
Today is the day to see a great change in your life.
Put your trust in Me and allow Me to work in you and through you.
I have seen the longing in your heart to go higher and higher in Me, and to walk with Me to the point where My Glory Light will fill you to overflow.
To the place where there is no darkness in you at all.
This is the place I AM calling all My children to come to.
That is where the true life will show forth and true power to overcome offence and come to the place in your life that no matter what has been done or said to you, it will not hurt you or move you to take offense.
I ask you to trust Me, and you will come to that place in your life.

John 8:12

Then spake Jesus again unto them, saying I AM the Light of the world.
He that followeth Me shall not walk in darkness, but shall have the Light of Life.

365 Day Devotional...God still speaks today...John 10:27

DAILY ENCOURAGING WORDS...*TO LIVE BY*

May 7th

Arise and shine for the Glory light of Jesus has come!
Let Me take over your life this day, surrender every part of your life to Me.
You don't just surrender one day, but everyday, for everyday is a new day.
You cannot live on yesterday's faith.
You need to cultivate your faith each day and walk with Me.
I AM always with you.
Sometimes you cannot feel Me, for you let things that are not from Me, come between us.
One on one, so that there will be no confusion as to what I want to relay to you and guide your way, you only need to surrender all to Me and trust Me.

Romans 1;17
For therein is the righteousness of God revealed from faith to faith, as it is written.
The just shall live by faith.

365 Day Devotional...God still speaks today...John 10:27

DAILY ENCOURAGING WORDS...*TO LIVE BY*

May 8th

Arise and shine for the Glory Light of Jesus has come!
Be still and know that I AM God.
Clear your mind of the things of this world and focus on Me.
When your mind is clear, My Holy Spirit will be able to give you clear directions on the things and problems that you have need of.
When you get so caught up on the things that are happening around you, there is no room for My Holy Spirit to move in and give your directions.
So, let go of the thoughts that just hammer at you, and ask My Holy Spirit to help you and guide you to give you the help that you need to conquer the problems that come against you.
The Holy Spirit has the Wisdom to lead you and give the answer that you need to solve all that you need answers and directions for.
Trust Me and praise Me and surrender all to Me this day.

John 14:26
But the Helper, the Holy Spirit whom the Father will send in My name, He will teach you all things and bring your remembrance, all that I have said to you.

365 Day Devotional...God still speaks today...John 10:27

DAILY ENCOURAGING WORDS...*TO LIVE BY*

May 9th

Arise and shine for the Glory Light of Jesus has come.
Peace be still My child.
Do not ponder, nor fret, all is well in My Hands.
When you are dealing with a situation and you see no improvement in what you have been seeking an answer for, do not give up but simply stand on My Word and receive it, for it is the power to overcome what you are dealing with.
Keep believing and receiving for it is yours.
Do not give p, the enemy of your soul is just waiting for you to do just that.
Do not give him the time of day, for you are My child and I will see you through.
You will overcome.
Speak forth My Word that lines up with what you want done in your life.
Stand firm and fight the good fight of Faith.
Be determined and do not give up.

Exodus 15:2
The Lord is my strength, and my song.
He has given me victory.

DAILY ENCOURAGING WORDS...*TO LIVE BY*

May 10

Arise and shine for the Glory Light of Jesus has come!
Let My Grace and Mercy flow into you this day.
My Grace is the Power to live victoriously over all the devil and what the world can bring against you.
Grace is the power to overcome, not to live a sloppy life before Me.
Some people are teaching that you can live your life and sin all you want to, this is not true, My Grace does not cover sins that are done knowingly and done repeatedly.
I long for My children to live for Me in truth and see that I loved them all, to die for them and was raised in resurrection power so that they could live a life of victory and become overcomers for Me.
That is the Power of My Grace for each and everyone.
So, I say unto you, walk in My Grace and be an overcomer.

Hebrews 4:16
Let us then with confidence draw near to the throne of Grace, that we may receive mercy and find Grace to help in time of need.

DAILY ENCOURAGING WORDS...*TO LIVE BY*

May 11th

Arise and shine for the Glory Light of Jesus has come!
Rest in Me, knowing that all is well in My Hands.
When you rest in Me, all the storms that come at you cannot touch you.
There is protection in Me.
You feel My Peace which is calmness.
That is where I want you to live your life out.
It is possible for you to do this when you keep your mind settled on Me and your eyes on Me.
This means you have put your whole attention directly on Me.
I want to be the central point in your life.
There is no room for the things of this world that does not have any life to offer.
I AM the way, the truth, and the life.
Outside of Me, there is no life that can satisfy you.
So, I say let Me be everything to you.

Romans 8:5
The mind governed by the flesh is death, but the mind governed by the Spirit is life and peace.

DAILY ENCOURAGING WORDS...*TO LIVE BY*

May 12th
Arise and shine for the Glory Light of Jesus has come!
Take courage and put your hand in Mine.
All is well and I will walk with you, and you will see the goodness of your God this day.
Let the joy rise in your heart and overtake you.
Rest in Me and I will work in your life.
I want to take you higher in Me, but you must be willing to lay aside the things of this world that weights heavy upon you.
They only keep you from growing in Me and becoming what I want you to be.
You do not have to walk alone; I AM with you.
Praise Me and put your trust in Me.
You can and will live in victory.
Look unto Me, the Author and finisher of your faith.
Go about your day for you are blessed.

Psalm 27:14
Wait on the Lord, be of good courage, and He shall strengthen thine heart.
Wait I say on the Lord.

365 Day Devotional...God still speaks today...John 10:27

May 13th

Arise and shine for the Glory Light of Jesus has come!
Step into My way of doing things.
They are totally opposite of the ways of the world.
When you live in the Spirit this is how you do things,
through the Holy Spirit.
The Holy Spirit will lead you in the way you should go and
the way you should do things.
The way of the world is to lead you into darkness and the
way of the Holy Spirit is to lead you into the Light, for He
is Light.
The things of this world is controlled by Satan.
The Kingdom of God is controlled by My Holy Spirit.
You cannot mix the two.
You choose one or the other.
I gave you a free will and I will not step over your will.
So, I say to you, choose wisely this day, whom you will serve.

Deuteronomy 30:19

*I call Heaven and earth to record this day against you (that)
I have set before you life and death, blessing and cursing;
therefore, choose life, that both thou and thy seed may live.*

DAILY ENCOURAGING WORDS...*TO LIVE BY*

May 14th

Arise and shine for the Glory Light of Jesus has come!
This is a great day of rejoicing.
My Hand is upon you and My love surrounds you.
I will carry you through your day, as you look to Me and expect Me to move on your behalf.
Believe in your heart and speak with your mouth victory in every part of your life.
I am interested in every part of your life.
I want you to be whole and living a life of victory.
There is My Power in you to bring you to wholeness.
Walk in My Strengths, My Love, Joy, and Peace everyday.
Draw strength from My Word.
It will renew your mind and heal your soul, and it will accomplish My will in you.
So, stand on My Word and believe in your heart and speak forth My Word with your mouth.
There is power in My word for every part of your life.
Go about your day and be Blessed!

Philippians 2:13
For it is God which worketh in you both to will and to do His good pleasure.

DAILY ENCOURAGING WORDS...*TO LIVE BY*

May 15th

Arise and shine for the Glory Light of Jesus has come!
Walk not in your own understanding.
Come to Me and ask for wisdom, knowledge and understanding, for I will give it to you.
You cannot walk in the ways of the world and expect to have the abundant life that I have for you.
When you seek Me, you will have a direction for your life and you will know what to do, to receive all I desire for you.
A life of freedom and power to live your life for Me, in abundance.
The life I have for you, is to be able to live in peace and for your life to touch others, by walking in My Love and by loving others as I have loved you.
Your life is to be a continual life living for Me and reaching out to others.
You are not to live only for yourself, there is no power in this.
As I gave My life for you, so will you give your life for others also, they will see the love of God working in you and through you, and this will draw others to Me.

Proverbs 3:5
Trust in the Lord with all your heart and lean not unto thine own understanding.

DAILY ENCOURAGING WORDS...*TO LIVE BY*

May 16th

Arise and shine for the Glory Light of Jesus has come!
Taste and see that the Lord is good.
Trust in Me and give to Me all that concerns you and weighs you down.
Do not let the load get so heavy that you feel that you cannot get out from under it.
This is where you cast your cares all unto Me.
I took all the things that trouble you onto Myself at the Cross of Calvary.
This is why I say surrender all to Me.
Just believe and receive this and trust that I will take care of all that concerns you.
I AM your burden bearer.
Learn to walk in freedom and in My Goodness.
If you carry the load, you are not in faith that I can and will take care of you.
Faith in Me is what moves Me to work in your life.
Hold nothing back.
I long for you to walk in all that I died for, so that you could enjoy your life to the fullness thereof

Nahum 1:7
The Lord is good, a stronghold in the day of trouble; and He knoweth them that trust Him.

DAILY ENCOURAGING WORDS...*TO LIVE BY*

May 17th

Arise and shine for the Glory Light of Jesus has come!
Trust in Me this day for I Am in it.
Know that you have all the power and strength from your God to go through anything that comes at you today.
Look to Me for everything.
I AM, not just in one part of your life, but I AM is in every part of your life.
You are made in the image of Me, so you are part of Me.
You have the DNA of Me in you.
This is why I call you to a higher lifestyle than what the world has.
You walk in My light, not in the darkness of this world.
Keep your eyes on Me and do not listen to all the voices that would try to tell you otherwise.
I AM the way, the Truth, and the Life.

John 14:6

Jesus saith unto him, I AM the way, the Truth and the Life, no man cometh unto the Father, but by Me.

DAILY ENCOURAGING WORDS...*TO LIVE BY*

May 18th

Arise and shine for the Glory Light of Jesus has come!
Go about your day and be blessed!
Know that I AM is with you, wherever you go and whatever you do.
Look to Me and ask for whatever you need for this day.
What ever you ask in My Name, faith believing, I will give it to you.
I long to bless My children, it blesses Me so.
Put your trust in Me and sing praises unto Me.
I will lead you and bring you through this day.
My eyes are always on you.
You are never alone for; I AM there with you.
You need not feel lonely.
Just ask and receive.

Mark 11:24

Therefore, I say unto you, what things soever ye desire, when ye pray, believe that ye receive them, and ye shall have them.

365 Day Devotional...God still speaks today...John 10:27

DAILY ENCOURAGING WORDS...*TO LIVE BY*

May 19th

Arise and shine for the Glory Light of Jesus has come!
Let Me into every part of your life.
I desire to make you whole.
I need your help and permission to work in you.
Unless you will allow Me to come in and do what must be done, so that you can grow and come into the place of maturity in your spiritual walk in Me, it is by choice.
The natural man does not want to walk in the Spirit for it wants nothing to do with the Spiritual life.
The Spirit cannot co-exist with the natural or the flesh part of man.
In the Spirit walk, there is no room for the flesh.
This is why you must choose which one you will walk in.
If you walk in the Spirit of God, you walk in faith and that causes the Hand of the Lord to work in you.
You cannot walk in both; it must be one or the other.

Galatians 5:1
Stand fast therefore in the liberty wherewith Christ hath made us free and be not entangled again with the yoke of bondage.

DAILY ENCOURAGING WORDS...*TO LIVE BY*

May 20th

Arise and shine for the Glory Light of Jesus has come!
Be still and know that I AM God.
As you go about your day, know that all is well.
Always look to Me for all that you need, for there is not another one that has the power to supply everything you need.
Your needs are Spiritual and physical, and emotional and financial.
I AM the ONE and ONE alone that can make you whole.
Be not deceived to think that mankind can make you whole.
Do not put your life in the hands of another, for it will cause you to stumble and put you off the path I put you on.
I have made a way for you and that way is through trust, believe and receive.
My ways are not hard, just apply yourself and be willing to take My written Word and stand on it, speak it forth.
This is My way.
I AM waiting on you.

Philippians 4:19
But my God shall supply all my needs according to His riches in Glory, by Christ Jesus.

DAILY ENCOURAGING WORDS...*TO LIVE BY*

May 21st

Arise and shine for the Glory Light of Jesus has come!
Be still and know that I AM God.
Put aside all the things that are going on in your life that does not glorify Me or builds you up in Me.
Anything that does not line up with My Word, has no value in your life.
It takes away from you, your faith walk and you become weak in your spirit.
They take over your time, time you should be building yourself up in My Word.
For that is where your strength comes from.
Time is a precious commodity that Satan would love to steal from you.
Do not allow him to do this but take control of your time and put it to good use.
Spend time in My presence and give Me Glory and thanksgiving and see what I will do for you.
Combine all these things along with My Word and you will become what I have called you to be.

Psalm 90:12
So, teach (us) to number our days, that we may apply (our) hearts unto wisdom.

DAILY ENCOURAGING WORDS...*TO LIVE BY*

May 22nd

Arise and shine for the Glory Light of Jesus has come!
Guard your heart, for out of it determines the course of your life.
How you act and what comes out of your mouth is what was in your heart all along.
You have the help of the Holy Spirit to tame your tongue.
No man can tame his tongue, but the Holy Spirit can and will if you give Him permission to do so.
You need to keep track of what is going on in your thoughts, in your mind.
They affect the decisions that you make.
Wrong thoughts will lead you to make wrong decisions.
Any negative thoughts are not of Me, for they will destroy you.
You can determine what is good or bad with the help of the Holy Spirit.
Ask Him to take over your thought life.
He is your helper.

Proverbs 4:23
Keep thy heart with all diligence, for out of it (are) the issues of life.

365 Day Devotional...God still speaks today...John 10:27

DAILY ENCOURAGING WORDS...*TO LIVE BY*

May 23rd

Arise and shine for the Glory Light of Jesus has come!
Let Me lead the way, for I see what is ahead of you.
When you walk close to Me you will not stumble for you are able to walk by My Light, for My light is there to show you the way.
I AM the Light so trust Me.
You will not walk in darkness as long as you stay close to Me.
When you take your eyes off Me, is when you become fearful, and your faith begins to waver.
When you allow fear in, then faith cannot work on your behalf.
Faith is full in you when you continually walk with Me.
Fear will paralyze you, so that you will not be able to walk with Me.
Do not give an open door for the enemy of your soul to come in but stand firm in My Word and praise Me and keep your eyes on Me.
I AM always there for you.

Isaiah 4:13
For I the Lord thy God will hold thy right hand, saying unto thee, fear not, I will help thee.

365 Day Devotional...God still speaks today...John 10:27

DAILY ENCOURAGING WORDS...*TO LIVE BY*

May 24th

Arise and shine for the Glory Light of Jesus has come!
Put your trust in Me and stand firm for righteousness.
No matter where you go or what you do, let your light shine for Me, in every situation, there is no middle road.
I have called you to walk the narrow path of life.
There is no room for things of the world nor the ways that things are done in this world.
Remember that you gave yourself to Me and I want to work in your life, so that you will be made whole and let your life show what I have done for you.
I want to use your life to let others see the goodness and faithfulness of God.
I AM almighty God and if you allow Me to be the only God in your life, I will do in you what I have already planned for you.
You will walk in My ways, and you will show forth the goodness of your God and be fulfilled in every area of your life.
Surrender to Me and see what I will do for you, I will not and cannot fail you.

Psalm 34:8
O taste and see that the Lord is good, blessed is the man that trusted in Him.

365 Day Devotional...God still speaks today...John 10:27

DAILY ENCOURAGING WORDS...*TO LIVE BY*

May 25th

Arise and shine for the Glory Light of Jesus has come!
Come into My presence and spend time with Me.
Let My presence saturates your whole being.
I AM is all that you need.
Look to Me and surrender all to Me.
It is not in your power to face and have the answers, that you need for all the situations in your life, but the power is in and through Me.
This power can dismantle all the situations that come your way that you cannot face alone.
It does not matter what these situations are.
Stay in My presence and ask for Me and trust Me, you will be able to live for Me, no matter what challenges you face.
I AM The ALL sufficient ONE, there is no other.
Praise Me and walk in faith and know that you are always in My presence.
It is possible to be in My presence for I live within you, through My Holy Spirit.

Psalm 16:11
Thou will show me the path of life.
In thy presence (is) fulness of joy, at thy hand (therefore) pleasures for evermore.

365 Day Devotional...God still speaks today...John 10:27

May 26th

Arise and shine for the Glory Light of Jesus has come!
Today is a great day of rejoicing.
Lift your head and sing unto your God.
Sing praises unto Me!
Expect the unexpectable!
Do you think that I AM cannot turn things around in your life and put things for you?
There is nothing that I do not see going on in your life that I can work on in your behalf.
Look to Me and know that your God is all-sufficient.
Draw strength from Me this day and do not look back, don't look ahead but look to Me and I will lead you and guide you and put you on a straight path that will bring Glory to Me.
I love you My child, all is well.

2nd Corinthians 12:9
And He said unto Me, My Grace is sufficient for thee, for My strength is made perfect in weakness.

DAILY ENCOURAGING WORDS...*TO LIVE BY*

May 27th

Arise and shine for the Glory Light of Jesus has come!
Come before Me this day with thanksgiving flowing out of your heart.
Be thankful for the Gift that flows from Me every moment of your day.
That is the Gift of Salvation, through the Blood that flowed from My body that day on the cross at Calvary.
I did this for all mankind.
This work will never fail for I can not fail.
My blood washes away all stains that sin leaves on you.
It can be washed away by the Blood of the Lamb.
I gave freely that day and I still freely give the Gift of life to all that will receive Me and the work of redemption.
The Gift of true life to all mankind.
Reach out today and share the love that flows in you and through you to all that are around you.
For truly I love you with an everlasting LOVE that cannot fail.

John 3:16
For God so loved the world, that He gave His only Son, that whosoever believeth in Hem should not perish, but have everlasting life.

365 Day Devotional...God still speaks today...John 10:27

DAILY ENCOURAGING WORDS...*TO LIVE BY*

May 28th

Arise and shine for the Glory Light of Jesus has come!
Keep your eyes on Me, for that is where the power comes from.
The minute you take your eyes off Me, is when you become fearful, you no longer see Me, but you turned your fucus on your situation at hand.
This clouds your mind so that you cannot think straight.
The enemy of your soul now has a foothold on your thoughts and can keep you in fear.
If you will turn inward and ask the Holy Spirit to help you get back on track and receive His help, then you are able to shut down the fear that the devil has trapped you in.
Begin to praise and give honour to Me and My Peace will flood your soul.
The more you praise Me, the devil will flee from you.
He cannot stand My children praising Me.
There is power in praise and thanksgiving.

Psalm 50:15
And call upon Me in the day of trouble.
I will deliver thee, and thou shall Glorify Me.

DAILY ENCOURAGING WORDS...*TO LIVE BY*

May 29th

Arise and shine for the Glory Light of Jesus has come!
Walk in confidence before Me.
Not confidence in yourself but the confidence in Me.
For without Me you can do nothing.
Only by the Holy Spirit which dwells in you can all things be accomplished.
Expect great things to come this day!
I move according to your faith so put your faith in Me.
Praise Me and always look to Me.
Keep Me on your Mind and in your heart.
When I AM on your mind, there will be no room for anything else to move in and lead you off your path to serving Me.
It is very important to keep your mind on the things that pertain to Me.
As you do this you will see your life change for the better, you will also become closer to Me.
This is the ultimate goal, to be changed into My image.
Trust Me and continue to walk with Me.
Go about your day for you are Blessed.

Philippians 4:9
Those things, which ye have both learned and received, and heard and seen in Me, do and the God of Peace shall be with you.

365 Day Devotional...God still speaks today...John 10:27

DAILY ENCOURAGING WORDS...*TO LIVE BY*

May 30th

Arise and shine for the Glory Light of Jesus has come!
Walk upright before Me.
I am calling My people to walk in My righteousness.
To let your life be free of things that are opposite to My ways.
I AM calling you to walk in My integrity in all that you do, so that your light will shine forth in every area of your life.
You are called by My Name, and you represent Me.
I want to show forth in your life, the best of Me so that others will see what I have done in your life, and they will know that I AM real, and they will want to have what you have.
Show forth your God through your lifestyle.
So, walk in My ways.
I love you, I long to see you, walking in My freedom and in My Joy, Peace, and My Love.

Psalm 15:23
He that walk uprightly, and worketh righteousness and speaketh the truth in his heart.

DAILY ENCOURAGING WORDS...*TO LIVE BY*

May 31st

Arise and shine for the Glory Light of Jesus has come!
Walk in the Light, for I AM the Light.
Take My Hand and walk with Me.
I will lead you and show you the way.
I will never leave you.
I already see the struggles that you go through.
Bring them all to Me and let Me show your how to deal with them.
I will pour My strength into you.
You do not have the kind of strength in your own ability to walk through your struggles alone.
You can trust Me and My strength will take you through.
My goal for you is to overcome everything that comes your way.
You will have many temptations.
If you only keep looking to Me, you will be able to overcome them all, for I AM with you.
Never doubt your walk with Me.
Keep Me always in your sight and in your Heart.

Hebrews 2:18
For in that He, Himself hath suffered being tempted.
He is able to succour them that are tempted.

DAILY ENCOURAGING WORDS...*TO LIVE BY*

JUNE

2nd Corinthians 9:8

And God is able to make all grace abound to you, so that always having all sufficiency in everything, you may have an abundance for every good deed;

DAILY ENCOURAGING WORDS...*TO LIVE BY*

June 1st

Arise and shine for the Glory Light of Jesus has come!
Hear Me when I say, look to Me for I Am your God.
I AM the one that brought you into existence and gave you life. I already planned your life from before the foundation of this world.
You are very dear to My Heart, and I love you with an everlasting Love.
My love is forever and is on a much higher level than the love of this world.
My Love will never fade, but the love of this world comes and goes, you cannot trust in it for it comes from your emotions, which are not stable.
So, forsake the love of this world and take hold of My Love and put your faith and trust in Me.
My Love is a stabilizer, and you can count on it.
It will keep you even in your everyday life if you will make up your mind that you will walk in My Love every moment of your day.
You can do this by the power of the Holy Spirit that is within you.

1st John 4:10

Here in is love, not that we loved God, but that He loved us, and sent His Son (to be) the propitiation for our sins.

365 Day Devotional...God still speaks today...John 10:27

DAILY ENCOURAGING WORDS...*TO LIVE BY*

June 2nd

Arise and shine for the Glory Light of Jesus has come!
Come to Me in the first part of your day.
I AM waiting on you to spend time with Me.
In this time spent with Me, will refresh you and it is your fuel for the day.
Let My Holy Spirit fill you up and let the fruit of the Holy Spirit be operating in your life.
When you spend time in My presence, you will be full of My Power and strength to go about your day, and you will be walking in My perfect will.
When you do not come to Me at the beginning of your day, you open doors to the devil to come in and cause chaos throughout your whole day.
So, I say come in faith believing and you will not be disappointed.
Never forget that I AM with you always and will never leave you.
Go about your day, you are Blessed!

Matthew 6:33
But seek ye first the Kingdom of God, and His righteousness, and all these things shall be added unto you.

365 Day Devotional...God still speaks today...John 10:27

DAILY ENCOURAGING WORDS...*TO LIVE BY*

June 3rd

Arise and shine for the Glory Light of Jesus has come!
Rejoice, rejoice, My child, for today is a Blessed day!
Allow Me to touch you this day.
I long to Bless you and change your life and bring you to a place in Me, that will cause you to see the goodness of Your God.
I long to have you work in My ways and you will see that your God is more willing to give you what you need and wants to give you the desires of your heart, more than you are willing to receive.
So, I say open your heart to Me and call upon My Name, and surrender all to Me so that I can move mightily in your life.
You do not have to live in lack and live below what I have and want to give you.
So, arise My child and learn of Me and trust Me to work in your life, and don't hold back any longer.
This is the day to make a decision to surrender all to Me.

Psalm 37:4
Delight thyself also in the Lord, and He shall give thee the desires of thine heart.

365 Day Devotional...God still speaks today...John 10:27

DAILY ENCOURAGING WORDS...*TO LIVE BY*

June 4th

Arise and shine for the Glory Light of Jesus has come!
Walk with a purpose this day.
Put your trust in Me and know that I AM with you.
Walk in My Love, Peace, and Joy.
Leave all to Me and walk in faith.
There is power in walking in My Love, Love conquers all.
No matter what situation you find yourself in.
The love of God overrides it.
There is nothing stronger than My Love, My Love is in you all the time.
All you need to do is be willing to turn your back on everything that is not of Me.
The enemy of your soul cannot stand it when you walk in My Love, for he knows that he cannot touch you.
So, when evil is done to you, overcome evil with good, always be looking for an opportunity to extend your hand to bless someone in My Love.
Just remember that My Love is the most powerful thing on earth!

1st John 4:6-7

Dear friends, let us love one another, for love comes from God. Everyone who loves has been born of God and knows God.

DAILY ENCOURAGING WORDS...*TO LIVE BY*

June 5th

Arise and shine for the Glory Light of Jesus has come!
Can you not see that when you ask for Me to do things in your life, to make you more like Me, this is when I go ahead and start a process to bring about that change that needs to be done?
I take circumstances and people to work in your life to bring forth the petition that you have put before Me.
Remember that it is done when you ask, believe, and receive what I will do for you.
The changes do not come overnight.
Be patient and let Me do what needs to be done.
I will take you from Glory to Glory.
You are changed little by little.
I know everything about you for I made you.
Put your faith in Me and completely trust Me to do what I want to do in you and through you.
You are My child and I love you with an everlasting heart.

Mark 11:24
Therefore, I say unto you, what things so ever ye desire, when you pray, believe that ye receive (them) and ye shall have (them).

365 Day Devotional...God still speaks today...John 10:27

DAILY ENCOURAGING WORDS...*TO LIVE BY*

June 6th

Arise and shine for the Glory Light of Jesus has come!
Let not your heart be troubled, for I see and know all things.
You can bring all to Me, what is on your mind and heart and know that I AM open to what you have to say.
Sometimes when you are troubled, it is hard to let go, but you need to surrender to Me and give Me all that is on your heart.
If you do not surrender to Me, you will not be able to have peace.
So, I say surrender all to Me and I will work on the situation that is troubling you.
Let faith arise in your heart and release all to Me.
I already know what troubles you.
You cannot keep Me from knowing for I know all things.
I AM on your side, and I AM always with you, nothing is impossible for Me.

Psalm 55:22
Cast your burden upon the Lord, and He shall sustain thee, He shall never suffer the righteous to be moved.

365 Day Devotional...God still speaks today...John 10:27

DAILY ENCOURAGING WORDS...*TO LIVE BY*

June 7th

Arise and shine for the Glory Light of Jesus has come!
Come unto Me, when you are weary, and I will give you rest.
Take time and spend the time away from everything and everyone, so that I can minister to you.
Your mind is so full of everything that you think you must do and is going around in circles to find the answers.
Surrender to Me, so I can put My Peace into your mind and heart.
Without My Peace operating in your life, you have no joy, and it is hard to operate in love.
I AM calling you to lay aside all the things that come at you, that cause you to fear and lose what peace you did have.
Remember that I AM a God of Peace, not fear.
Don't allow the enemy to steal what I have given you.
Always put Me first and I will keep you in perfect Peace.
When you are in My Peace, I can Bless you, then you will walk in My Joy and Love.
So, come to Me before you start your day.
You truly will see a great difference in your life.

Philippians 4:7
And the peace of God, which passeth all understanding, shall keep your hearts and minds through Christ Jesus

DAILY ENCOURAGING WORDS...*TO LIVE BY*

June 8th

Arise and shine for the Glory Light of Jesus has come!
Taste and see the Goodness of the Lord.
When you look upon Me and when you read about Me in My written Word, you learn different aspects of Me.
How I had compassion on the people that were afflicted with all manner of disease and illness.
I healed the lame, opened the blind eyes, and opened deaf ears; I am the same today as I was then.
You are My Hands now here on earth.
I have commissioned you to go forth and heal the sick and set the captives free from Satan's hold on them.
I have given you the power to do so.
The Holy Spirit with you is that power.
Allow Him to flow through you and lead you to do the works that I did and even greater works than I did.
Do not be afraid, only believe what I have said and what is written in My Word.
There is power in My written Word to heal, for those who would believe and stand on My Word to do what is said
Take it by faith and you will receive this power

Matthew 10:8
Heal the sick, cleanse the lepers, raise the dead, cast out devils, freely ye have received, freely give.

365 Day Devotional...God still speaks today...John 10:27

DAILY ENCOURAGING WORDS...*TO LIVE BY*

June 9th

Arise and shine for the Glory Light of Jesus has come!
Let Me be the one to orchestrate what is happening in your life.
You are too close to the situation, to totally understand and cannot see all that is behind it, if you will trust that I can and will do a shift change in your whole situation.
Just remember that I can take the bad and turn it around for the good.
I keep watch over you and all that concerns you.
You can get side tracked which takes your eyes off Me.
When you allow this, you start to lose hope and think that situations are getting out of hand.
I say My child, keep your eyes on Me and believe that I will do what needs to be done concerning you.
Do not let your faith waiver but stay strong.
Keep trusting in Me and know that I will never fail you.

Romans 8:28
And we know that all things work together for good to them that love God, to them who are the called according to His purpose.

DAILY ENCOURAGING WORDS...*TO LIVE BY*

June 10th

Arise and shine for the Glory Light of Jesus has come!
Put your trust in Me no matter what is happening around you.
You are safe in the protection of My Power.
I have sent the Host of Heaven, My warring Angles to keep guard over you.
They go wherever you go.
You also have a Guardian Angle that is with you all the time.
So, you need not fear.
You also have the Holy Spirit within you to help you and guide you in the way you should go.
So, walk out your life knowing that all is well, and you are in the Palm of My Hand.
I watch over you, My eyes are always on you.
Be mindful that you are never alone.
Have a thankful heart and praise Me, put Me first in your life to see what I will do for you.

Psalm 91:11
For He shall give His Angels charge over thee, to keep thee in all thy ways.

365 Day Devotional...God still speaks today...John 10:27

DAILY ENCOURAGING WORDS... *TO LIVE BY*

June 11th

Arise and shine for the Glory Light of Jesus has come!
When you let go and surrender all to Me, this shows Me that you trust Me with all.
I will do what needs to be done concerning you.
I long for My children to come to Me with everything that concerns them.
There is nothing too small or to overwhelming for Me.
Remember I see the beginning and the end, and everything in between.
I can put things back in order and put you back on track.
I am interested in every part of your life.
I want you whole and living the life that I have planned for you.
A life that shows forth My Love, that flows from within you, always reaching out to others, always putting others before yourself.
This is in resemblance of Me.

Psalm 37:5
Commit thy way unto the Lord; trust also in Him, and He shall bring (it) to pass.

365 Day Devotional...God still speaks today...John 10:27

June 12th

Arise and shine for the Glory Light of Jesus has come!
Walk in My likeness.
Old things have passed away and all things have become new.
You no longer look to the ways of the world, but to the ways that I do things.
Surrender your life completely to Me, so that I can teach you My ways and then you will begin to change and think the way I think and the way I do things.
You are made in My image, so therefore you are made into the likeness of Me.
I have put everything in you, so that you can and will overcome the things that have held you back.
I say this is a new day and you will walk according to the way I have for you.
Look to no other, only to Me, I am everything that you need.
Renew your mind by the washing of My Word and let it sink deep into your heart, so that you will be able to stand on it and grow from Glory to Glory, trust Me in all that you do.

Psalm 32:8

I will instruct thee and teach thee in the way which thow shall go. I will guide thee with Mine eye.

DAILY ENCOURAGING WORDS...*TO LIVE BY*

June 13th

Arise and shine for the Glory Light of Jesus has come!
Reach out to Me and open your heart to let Me in to every part of your life.
I keep knocking at your heart's door, wanting you to open and let Me in.
I cannot come in until you give Me permission to do so.
I will not cross man's will.
When I created man, I gave him a free will.
You must make the choice, whether to open the door of your heart to Me.
I went to the Cross and died for all mankind.
I rose the third day and now I AM seated at the right hand of the Father.
My Holy Spirit lives inside of you, waiting to bring you to the place of fulfillment in every part of your life.
It is your choice.
What will it be, life or death?
Choose this day.

Deuteronomy 30:19
I call heaven and earth to record this day against you, that I have set before you life and death, blessing and cursing's, therefore choose life that both thou and thy seed may live.

365 Day Devotional...God still speaks today...John 10:27

DAILY ENCOURAGING WORDS...*TO LIVE BY*

June 14th

Arise and shine for the Glory Light of Jesus has come.
Go about your day and be Blessed.
Know that I AM is with you wherever you go and whatever you do.
Look to me and ask for whatever you need for this day.
Whatever you ask in My Name, faith believing, I will give it to you.
Do not ask amiss.
Ask according to My will and it shall be done unto you.
I long to Bless My children, it Blesses Me so.
Put your trust in Me and sing praises unto Me.
I will lead you and bring you through this day.
My eyes are always on you.
You are never alone, for I AM there with you.
You need not feel lonely, just ask, and receive.

Mark 11:24
Therefore, I say unto you, what things soever ye desire, when ye pray, believe that you receive them, and ye shall have them.

DAILY ENCOURAGING WORDS...*TO LIVE BY*

June 15th

Arise and shine for the Glory Light of Jesus has come!
Be not downcast, because the hope of Glory lives in the inside of you.
In Him is all in all.
Draw from Him this day and know that whatever you need is there.
The strength that is needed is in Him.
Praise Him and lift Him up in song and let your thoughts be on Him.
This is the way you release whatever you need from Him.
He loves you and wants to be in your life everyday.
Seek Him in all that you do.
He is always with you.
He will never leave you nor forsake you.
Go about your day and know that all is well.

Colossians 1:27
To whom God would make known what is the riches of the Glory of this mystery among the Gentiles, which is Christ in you, the hope of Glory.

DAILY ENCOURAGING WORDS...*TO LIVE BY*

June 16th

Arise and shine for the Glory Light of Jesus has come!
Let Me show you the way that you need to walk in.
It has already been arranged by Me.
It is not a hard path, when you rely on My Holy Spirit, who is your leader and guide.
He goes before you to make the crooked path straight for you.
You will never get lost unless you take your eyes off Me.
If you take your eyes off Me, then you take yourself off the path of life that has been set before you.
Only trust in the Holy Spirit and lean on Him for everything that you need to know.
Fill yourself up with My Word, for it is the sustainer for your life.
Feed daily on My Word, it will keep you strong and will show you the way to go and what to do.
The Holy Spirit and My Word work together.
Do not rely on yourself but work along with the Holy Spirit.
You will never go wrong

Ezekiel 36:37

And I will put My Spirit within you and cause you to walk in My statutes, and ye shall keep My judgments and do them.

DAILY ENCOURAGING WORDS...*TO LIVE BY*

June 17th

Arise and shine for the Glory Light of Jesus has come!
You see how it is so important to walk in Love?
If you allow strife to come in, then you are cutting off your faith.
Faith is the power, and the love compels it.
They work hand in hand.
So be careful to be diligent to be always on guard.
Strife always opens the door for your enemy (Satan) to bring all kinds of things that is not good to afflict your life.
Allow Me to fill you up daily, so that you will always walk in My presence.
It is possible to be able to always live in Me, this is what I want you to do, to bring you to a place where you always live in My presence.
How you do this is to constantly keep your eyes on Me.
If your eyes are on Me, then there is no room for anything else to take over.
Let My name be on your lips and praises come from your heart, worship unto Me.

Ephesians 4:26
Be ye angry and sin not, let not the sun go down upon your wrath.

DAILY ENCOURAGING WORDS...*TO LIVE BY*

June 18th

Arise and shine for the Glory Light of Jesus has come!
Walk close to Me and commune with Me.
Tell Me what is on your heart, My ear is always open to listen, you are very special to Me.
You can tell Me everything that is causing your heartaches.
As you tell Me, it is a release for you.
As you surrender all to Me, you will sense the heaviness leave you.
There is power in your words.
As you release the matters of your soul, that power begins to work in you, and you are then released from the weight that was weighing you down.
Let the Holy Spirit work in you to set you free.
He is the power that works in your life.
As you allow him to do so, He will do the work that is needed in your life.
He is always with you, He is your helper, so call on Him to help you.
You will then grow in your walk with Me, always going forward.

Galatians 5:25
If we live in the Spirit, let us also walk in the Spirit.

DAILY ENCOURAGING WORDS...*TO LIVE BY*

June 19th

Arise and shine for the Glory Light of Jesus has come!
This is a new day, walk in My purity.
I shed My blood so that you would be washed from all your sins and purified by the washing of My Blood.
Old things are passed away and you become a new creature in Me, therefore, the past has been forgiven.
You now walk in the fullness of what I have done for you.
So, I say, do not dwell in your past, for in My eyes your past is gone.
If you do not believe this, then you will always be looking to the past and it will surely bring you into bondage.
This is not what I died for.
I did so that you could be free and walking in My Light, not the darkness of your past.
Take heart and know that if you will surrender all to Me, and truly believe that I forgave you of your past, then the power of the past over you will be broken and you will be set free to walk completely in My Light.
Choose Light, not darkness.

1st John 3:3
And every man that hath this hope in Him, purifieth himself even as He is pure.

365 Day Devotional...God still speaks today...John 10:27

DAILY ENCOURAGING WORDS...*TO LIVE BY*

June 20th

Arise and shine for the Glory Light of Jesus has come!
My child, I AM calling you to a higher level in Love.
Love is the key to walk out your life in Me.
Love is always giving of yourself, to help others.
I AM love.
I want all My children to walk in love, so that the world will be able to see Me in you.
There is no true love coming out of the world.
So, you see how important it is for you to walk in love with all whom you meet.
To walk in My Love, is to watch what you speak.
If you are speaking unkind words to someone, then you are honouring the enemy of your soul.
If you confess to be a follower of Me, people will not see Me, in you.
There are only two sides to the spiritual.
One side is darkness and the other is Light.
Always let your Light shine before all mankind.
Honor Me through your words, also through your actions.
Walk in love.

1st John 4:7

Beloved, let us love one another, for love is of God, and everyone that loveth is born of God, and knoweth God.

DAILY ENCOURAGING WORDS...*TO LIVE BY*

June 21st

Arise and shin for the Glory Light of Jesus has come!
Bask in My Light.
I AM Light.
My Light is My presence, in doing so you will become stronger.
This is where My Holy Spirit will fill you up.
Surrender your time and will to bask in My presence.
It is also where you get your peace and joy.
They are the fruit of the Holy Spirit.
It is important to draw from the Holy Spirit daily.
This is where your strength and power come from.
Your spiritual walk will grow daily, as you do this.
You work as a team with the Holy Spirit.
He is within you; He is always waiting on you.
So, allow yourself to be open and to trust the Holy Spirit.
He will never let you down.
Spend time with Him and you will see yourself flourish in the things of Me.
Lift Him up in praise and worship throughout your day.

Jude 1:20
But ye, yourselves on your most Holy faith, praying in the Holy Spirit.

365 Day Devotional...God still speaks today...John 10:27

DAILY ENCOURAGING WORDS...*TO LIVE BY*

June 22nd

Arise and shine for the Glory Light of Jesus has come!
I am pleased with you, My child.
I have watched over you and I see your desire to lay everything down that is not of Me.
When you do so, you are saying unto Me, that you surrender all.
This is what I call for from My children; to abandon all that would not be a help in their walk with Me.
It does not take much to catch you off guard to follow the things of this world, that would destroy your life in Me.
So, you see, that keeping your eyes and heart open to Me, you will stay on track.
Always remember to be willing to let go and let Me have My way in you.
Keep your mind clear of anything that would lead you away from Me, it all starts in the mind.
Always beware what is in your mind and keep it clear of all thoughts that would destroy your walk with Me.
You have been given the power to accomplish this

Romans 12:2

And be not conformed to this world; but be transformed by the renewing of your mind, that ye may prove what is that good, and acceptable, and perfect, will of God.

365 Day Devotional...God still speaks today...John 10:27

DAILY ENCOURAGING WORDS...*TO LIVE BY*

June 23rd

Arise and shine for the Glory Light of Jesus has come!
As I walk with you, you will know that I am with you, guiding your footsteps so that you will not stumble off the path.
This path is narrow but My Light shines on this path to show you the way.
Leave behind all the heavy burdens that weigh you down.
Put them at the foot of the cross and leave them there.
My way is easy and light.
I will never leave you, nor forsake you, so you need not be concerned about your burdens.
I am always with you, be not afraid.
Know as long as you keep your eyes on Me, all is well.
This is where you put your full trust in Me.
All will fall into place, for I know all that is going on, for I was the ONE that planned your life from the beginning.
So, when you follow the ONE that knows, you will not fall away.
Believe Me when I say that ALL is well, My child.

Isaiah 30:21
And thine ears shall hear a word behind thee, saying.
This (is) the way, walk ye in it.
When ye turn to the right hand, and when ye turn to the left.

DAILY ENCOURAGING WORDS...*TO LIVE BY*

June 24th

Arise and shine for the Glory Light of Jesus has come!
Be still and know that I AM God.
I see what is going on in you, I know your hearts desire and that your heart is turned toward Me.
I know the struggles that you go through.
Just remember to lean on Me and ask for My help in time of need.
I AM always there for you.
I cannot move on your behalf if you do not bring your cares and struggle to Me.
When you do this, then I can move on your behalf, and start to work things out for you.
Take one day at a time and start to tell Me all that concerns you, co-partner with Me and see how things will come together for you.
Know that I do all things well and you need not fret for you are in My Hands.
Take heart and know that ALL is well.

Psalm 9:10
Those who know Your Name trust in You, for You Lord have never forsaken those who are Yours.

365 Day Devotional...God still speaks today...John 10:27

DAILY ENCOURAGING WORDS...*TO LIVE BY*

June 25th

Arise and shine for the Glory Light of Jesus has come!
Walk in My fullness this day.
My fullness is in My Spirit; the Holy Spirit that abides inside of you.
He has the answers to all things that would arise in your life.
He is all knowing and all powerful.
He is always with you. When you are going through a difficult time, you do not have to seek out the answer but only ask the Holy Spirit to help you and lead you.
He is no respecter of persons.
He only needs you to surrender to Him and be willing to let Him work in you.
It does not matter what you need, He is there for you.
He is your Helper, Guide, Comforter, and Teacher.
Learn to depend on the Holy Spirit, He is your friend.
He goes wherever you go.
He will never leave you nor forsake you.
Trust Him for all things. you have not because you ask not.
Work with the Holy Spirit and see those changes for the good, develop in your life.

John 14;16

And I will pray to the Father, and He shall give you another comforter, that He may abide with you forever.

DAILY ENCOURAGING WORDS...*TO LIVE BY*

June 26th

Arise and shine for the Glory Light of Jesus has come!

Stand upright before Me.

This is an art of living before Me, that you can learn the ways of doing so.

The art is to learn to listen to My Holy Spirit.

If you are willing to do so, He is willing to teach you how to walk upright before Me.

You will put aside all things that would hinder you from giving your full attention to the Holy Spirit.

Take the time to spend in His presence and open to Him.

As you do so, you will begin to hear His still small voice.

It is important to train yourself to hear Him no matter where you are and what you are doing.

This is a matter of keeping your mind clear from the thoughts that would stop you from being able to hear Him.

He is always talking so you must always be listening for Him.

The two of you will become one, you will learn to trust Him in all your ways.

Matthew 11:15

He that have ears to hear, let him hear.

DAILY ENCOURAGING WORDS...*TO LIVE BY*

June 27th

Arise and shine for the Glory Light of Jesus has come!

This is a new day.

Be prepared to walk in the Spirit.

Wherever you go there is darkness all around you.

You wrestle not against flesh and blood but against principalities, against powers, against the rulers of darkness of the world, against spiritual wickedness in high places.

Put on the belt of Truth, breastplate of Righteousness, the shoes of Peace, shield of Faith, to quench the fiery darts of the wicked, put on the Helmet of Salvation and the Sword of the Spirit.

You walk in the Spirit so be dressed in the Holy Spirit to fight the darkness.

Do not fear the darkness but walk in the Light.

I AM the Light and the Light swallows up the darkness.

Follow Me and know that I AM with you, and I will never leave you, and I will fight for you.

Heed My Words and do as I have directed you to do, and you will overcome all things.

Trust Me and follow the Light.

John 8:12

Then Spake Jesus again unto them, saying; I AM the Light of the world. He that followeth Me shall not walk in the darkness but shall have the Light of life.

June 28th

Arise and shine for the Glory Light of Jesus has come!
Do you not know that the God of the whole world is looking down upon you and knows everything about you?
I created you for a higher calling than living from day to day.
I have called you out of darkness into My Glorious Light.
In My Light there is everything that life needs for you to have to live in the calling I have for you.
I have called you to love one another and to reach out beyond yourself and touch those around you and everywhere you go; with My Love.
I AM coming for a bride that is without spot or wrinkles, that is why you must come up to a higher place in Me.
Surrender all that keeps you from going higher in Me.
I will do the work in you that needs to be done.
I love you and you are very precious to Me.

1st Corinthians 13:4
Charity suffereth long and is kind
Charity envies not
Charity vaunteth not itself, is not puffed up.

DAILY ENCOURAGING WORDS...*TO LIVE BY*

June 29th

Arise and shine for the Glory Light of Jesus has come!
As you walk along the path of life, you will experience a lot of things.
You will have highs and lows in your life, but no matter what they are, know that I am with you.
I have already put within you all that you need.
I have given you My written Word which is powerful and will never fail you.
You walk in faith knowing that you can trust My Holy Spirit to show you the way in which you need to go.
You will enjoy My presence and walk in My Light.
When Satan tries to get you off your faith walk in Me, you rely on My written Word to stop him in his tracks.
My Word is powerful when you put it deep into your spirit.
You release it by faith, and it will accomplish what it has been sent to do.
The more you spend time in My Word, you will become strong, and your heart will be full of Love, Joy, and Peace.
These are powerful to you for a long and strong life in Me.

John 15:3
Now you are clean through the Word which I have spoken to you.

DAILY ENCOURAGING WORDS...*TO LIVE BY*

June 30th

Arise and shine for the Glory Light of Jesus has come!
Come and go with Me into My secret place.
There you will be protected and safe from the onslaughts of the enemy of your soul (Satan).
He is always trying to get your attention, so he can get you to step off your spiritual walk.
But I will lead you all the way through, if only you will depend on My Holy Spirit to lead you and teach you how to live out your Spiritual walk of life.
You are powerless to do it by yourself.
The enemy of your soul loves to tell you that you can do things by yourself.
He is a liar; he will lead you to doing the things of the world and not My ways.
Trusting the Holy Spirit for the truth of My Word and how it will lead you in the Spirit.
As you trust the Holy Spirit, you will grow more each day.
So, deny yourself and trust only in Me and My ways.
Walk in the Spirit and not in the flesh.

Galatians 5:16
(This) I say then, walk in the Spirit and ye shall not fulfill the lust of the flesh.

DAILY ENCOURAGING WORDS...*TO LIVE BY*

JULY

Psalm 92:12

The righteous man will flourish like the palm tree,

He will grow like a cedar in Lebanon.

365 Day Devotional...God still speaks today...John 10:27

DAILY ENCOURAGING WORDS...*TO LIVE BY*

July 1st

Arise and shine for the Glory Light of Jesus has come!
Walk in the goodness of your God.
I AM with you every moment of your day.
I never leave you; I AM just waiting for you to lean on Me
for all that you need in your day.
Set your mind upon Me and keep Me in the center of
everything that you are doing.
If you do this, you will have a clear path before you.
I will go before you and remove the obstacles that would
keep you from stumbling.
So, you see how important it is to keep a close check on
what is going on in your mind, all the time?
If unchecked, it is an open door for Satan to enter in and
have his way with you.
So, be aware always to what is going on in your mind.

Romans 12:2

And be not conformed to this world, be ye transformed by
the renewing of your mind, that ye may prove what (is,) that
good, and acceptable, and perfect, will of God.

DAILY ENCOURAGING WORDS...*TO LIVE BY*

July 2nd

Arise and shine for the Glory Light of Jesus has come!
If you walk in My ways, you will not walk in the flesh.
The flesh is selfish and out to control you in every way.
I AM love and I want My children to represent Me in Love,
concerning everything in their life.
You already have My love living inside of you.
So, let My love flow out of you.
Surrender all to Me so that My love can work in you and
flow through you.
When it flows through you, it will touch other people's lives
that are around you.
My love is not burdensome, for the joy of the Lord, it flows
out from My love.
It is uplifting and light, there is no darkness at all.
So, let My love flow freely this day.

1st John 4:7

Beloved, let us love one another; for love is of God, and everyone that loveth is born of God, and knoweth God.

DAILY ENCOURAGING WORDS...*TO LIVE BY*

July 3rd

Arise and shine for the Glory Light of Jesus has come!
Listen for My voice, it is very important that you be still so you can hear what I have to say to you.
Your walk is a spiritual walk, and you need to let the Holy Spirit speak to you, so He can tell you what you need to make you strong in your walk with Me.
You cannot do it by yourself.
If you try to do it by yourself, you are walking in the flesh.
The flesh and the Spirit cannot work together.
They are against each other.
The flesh follows the ways of the world, and the Spirit follows the things pertaining to Me.
You need to put down the flesh and work with the Holy Spirit to bring real life and joy and peace into your life.
If you do this, you will experience the life that I want you to have.
It is a choice that you alone can make.

Galatians 5:17

For the flesh lusteth against the Spirit, and the Spirit against the flesh, and these are contrary the one to the other, so that ye cannot do the things that ye would.

July 4th

Arise and shine for the Glory Light of Jesus has come!
I will lead you and be with you in all that you do.
As you learn to walk with Me and put your trust in Me, you will see the Hand of the Lord more and more in your life.
When you give up your life for Mine, all things of the world will begin to fall away, and you will begin to see the difference in yourself, and the Glory Light will shine in and through you and out to those around you.
That is My desire for you, to live a life of peace, joy, and righteousness.
So, I say lay down your life and take Mine.
I will always be there for you.

Joshua 1:9
Have I not commanded thee? Be strong and of good courage; be not afraid, neither be thou dismayed; for the Lord thy God is with thee whithersoever thou goest.

DAILY ENCOURAGING WORDS...*TO LIVE BY*

July 5th

Arise and shine for the Glory Light of Jesus has come!
Let Me be the mainstay in your life.
You can trust Me in all parts of your life.
No matter what it is I have the answer.
Since I will never leave you nor forsake you, I AM always waiting on you to call out My name and confide in Me.
There is nothing to great or so enormous, that I can not handle.
I am a loving God, and I love you with an unfailing love.
Never think that you can not come to Me.
You are My child, and I would never turn My back on you.
My arms are outstretched to you, run into them My child.
You are never alone.

Psalm 91:15
He shall call upon Me, and I will answer him.
I will be with him in troubles; I will deliver him and honor him.

DAILY ENCOURAGING WORDS...*TO LIVE BY*

July 6th

Arise and shine for the Glory Light of Jesus has come!

This day is a blessed day.

When you keep your mind stayed on Me, no other force can penetrate your mind.

Learn to fix your mind upon Me and the things that are connected to Me.

Your mainstay is the written Word.

My Word is truth and will never change, for I never change.

I am the same yesterday, today and forever.

You can believe and be grounded in Me and stay strong to the end.

Stay focussed on Me.

Lean not to the left nor to the right but straight ahead.

Let not your eyes wander but keep them on Me.

Let My Holy Spirit help you to do these things.

He is your guide, so that you can stay on track.

He is always with you.

Ephesians 6:10

Finally, my brothers, be strong in the Lord, and in the power of His Might.

July 7th

Arise and shine for the Glory Light of Jesus has come!
Take joy in the One who loves you and upholds you in the palm of His hand.
Take courage and praise and honour Me today.
As you walk in me, nothing can touch you.
There is peace, joy, and love, always living inside of you.
As you praise Me, you cause the love, joy, and peace to be activated inside of you to live for Me.
It is the Holy Spirit inside of you that helps you walk in the pathway I have put you on.
A path that will honour Me and cause you to have a glorious life and to walk in the power of the Holy Spirit.
Be blessed this day My children.

Romans 15:13

Now the God of Hope fill you with all joy and peace in believing, that ye may abound in hope, through the power of the Holy Spirit.

DAILY ENCOURAGING WORDS...*TO LIVE BY*

July 8th

Arise and shine for the Glory Light of Jesus has come.
Learn to walk in the Spirit.
It is so important that My children learn to let go of the carnal mind and that way of life.
To walk with Me, you will need to leave the carnal ways behind (the world ways of living) and surrender your life to My Holy Spirit, to help you to live totally for Me.
You cannot combine the two for they cannot work together.
I have called you out of this world and put you into My Kingdom, the Kingdom of Light.
There is no room for darkness.
When you are willing to surrender yourself to Me, the sooner you will live the way you are called to live, and change will start to take place.
There will be a mighty shift in you.
You will be able to see it, feel it and walk in it.
You will begin to walk in peace, and joy.
This is My will for you.

Micah 6:8

He hath showed thee, o man that (is) good, and what doth the Lord require of thee, but to do justly, and to love mercy, and to walk humbly with thy God.

DAILY ENCOURAGING WORDS...*TO LIVE BY*

July 9th

Arise and shine for the Glory Light of Jesus has come!
Let us go beyond what we think and realize that it is the Holy Spirit that knows all things.
So, why waste your time, to figure out the answers on your own.
The very thing that you think is the answer, really is way off and you cannot fix the situation without the Holy Spirit helping you.
He is with you if you just spend time with Him and tell Him your situation.
He without a doubt will show you what the answer is and it will not be hard to put into action.
He will lead you into truth.
You need to be always open to Him, so that He can pour into you peace, that keeps you settled within our own spirit.

John 15;26
But when the Comforter is come, whom I will send unto you from the Father, even the Spirit of Truth, which proceedeth from the Father, He shall testify of Me.

DAILY ENCOURAGING WORDS...*TO LIVE BY*

July 10th

Arise and shine for the Glory Light of Jesus has come!
Let not your heart be troubled, for I AM with thee.
It is time to put your life completely in My Hands.
Trusting Me each day.
I watch over you every moment of the day and night.
I know what will be coming into your day, and you will need to be ready to stop the enemy (Satan) from taking over your mind, for that is where he will try to hinder you from walking out your destiny.
He does not want you to be the overcomer that you are in Me.
You need to be built up with My Word so that you can speak My Word and put your enemy to flight.
He cannot stand up to My Word.
You can make him flee just like I did in the wilderness.
I overcame by the Word of God.
Speak it forth over your situation that comes your way.
Trust in Me and My Word for I was the Word before I became flesh and blood.

John 1:1

In the beginning was the Word, and the Word was with God, and the Word was God.

DAILY ENCOURAGING WORDS...*TO LIVE BY*

July 11th

Arise and shine for the Glory Light of Jesus has come!
Let go and let God have His way in your life.
There is nothing that is more important than what I have called you for and the plans I have already put in place for you.
The only thing that would hinder those plans is yourself.
You cannot give Me some of your life and keep what you think would be all right to keep.
I gave all, for you and I expect you to give all for Me.
You cannot walk out a righteous life for Me and hold onto the ways of this world.
Do you no know that Light and darkness cannot mix?
You either live in one or the other.
Choose this day which one you will live for and give yourself to it.
You cannot live in a lukewarm state and expect to be Blessed by Me.

Proverbs 23.26
My son, give Me thine heart, and let thine eyes observe My ways.

365 Day Devotional...God still speaks today...John 10:27

DAILY ENCOURAGING WORDS...*TO LIVE BY*

July 12th

Arise and shine for the Glory Light of Jesus has come!
Come and see what I have for you.
All that I have is yours.
Whatever you need for your life is found in Me.
You can access anything you need from My Word.
Take time from your day and spend in My Word.
When you do this, you are spending time with Me.
My Word will uplift you when you are down.
When you are weary, it will give you strength.
If you are overwhelmed, it will calm you down.
It will teach you how to walk in My Love, Joy, and Peace.
The fruit of the Holy Spirit is already inside of you, just waiting to be released in you.
You need to develop these fruits.
Spend time in Me so that the fruit of the Holy Spirit will mature in you.
Embrace the Word and embrace Me, for we are one and the same.

Galatians 5:22-23

But the fruit of the Spirit is love, joy, peace, longsuffering, gentleness, goodness, faith. Meekness, temperance; against such there is no law.

365 Day Devotional...God still speaks today...John 10:27

DAILY ENCOURAGING WORDS...*TO LIVE BY*

July 13th

Arise and shine for the Glory Light of Jesus has come!
Do not look upon your situation and think that there is no hope or help to see it change around for the good.
Ony I can see the whole picture and in doing so, only I can solve it.
I always take a bad situation and turn it around for good.
Just give it all to Me and see what I will do.
If you will be faithful and not give up, you will see a significant change in your situation.
Continue to give Me Praise and Honor and lift your eyes to look upon Me, for I AM your helper in times of need.
I long for My children to come to Me in times like this, knowing that I would never turn them away.

Psalm 121:1
I will lift up mine eyes unto the hills, from whense cometh my help.

DAILY ENCOURAGING WORDS...*TO LIVE BY*

July 14th

Arise and shine for the Glory Light of Jesus has come!
Let go and let God have His way.
To live totally for Me, you need to let go of all your ideas and dreams that do not line up with what I want for you.
When you let go and let Me work in you to fulfill what I have already planned for you, when you walk in My plan, all will come together for good in every part of your life.
What I have for you is always good and not for evil.
There is no evil in Me, so therefore all is well.
It is a walk of faith in Me, fulfilling your life to the fullest.
I don't leave things undone.
I always fulfill all that I have said over you.
We will walk together, and you will see the goodness that I have already prepared for you.

2nd Samuel 7:25

And no, O Lord God's the Word that Thou hast spoken concerning thy servant, and concerning his house, establish it for ever, and do as thou hast said.

DAILY ENCOURAGING WORDS...*TO LIVE BY*

July 15th

Arise and shine for the Glory Light of Jesus has come!
Walk with Me in the stillness of your mind.
Take thought of what is going on in your mind and weigh the thoughts to what would be honourable or disruptive in your walk with Me.
If it is not upright, it is planted there by the enemy (Satan) to stop the flow of what I want you to think about.
If it is not of Me, it can shift the whole balance of your walk with Me.
You will begin to go off track and will hardly notice it.
It would not be long, and things will begin to change, and you will slowly drift away from Me.
Thoughts are very powerful and what you think upon is where your mind will follow.
Be diligent and aware of what goes on in your mind and be Master of It to dispel all that is not of Me.

Philippians 2:5
Let this mind be in you, which also in Christ Jesus.

365 Day Devotional...God still speaks today...John 10:27

DAILY ENCOURAGING WORDS...*TO LIVE BY*

July 16th

Arise and shine for the Glory Light of Jesus has come!
Do not look to yourself for the answers that you need, for you will surely fail.
There is One that has the answers to all what you need.
I AM, the one, that is all knowing and see way beyond what you can see.
I see the barriers and obstacles that have been put into your pathway.
You cannot see them.
If you put your trust in Me and ask of Me, I will move them, so that you will be able to walk clearly on your path that I have laid out before you.
You were never meant to do things on your own.
Put aside all things that would make you think that you could do on your own.
You are not strong enough to do this.
If you were, you would not need Me.
Look to the One that loves you and cares about your life.
Move forward in Me.

John 14: 13-14

And whatsoever ye shall ask in My Name, that will I do, that the Father may be Glorified in the Son.

365 Day Devotional...God still speaks today...John 10:27

DAILY ENCOURAGING WORDS...*TO LIVE BY*

July 17th

Arise and shine for the Glory Light of Jesus has come!
Take My Hand and I will lead you in the way you should go.
Aways trust Me and let Me show you what I want for you.
For that to happen, you must let go of all the things in the pas, that have kept you from going forward.
Only you can free yourself, by letting go of the hurts and forgive the ones that hurt you.
If you are willing to do this, you will be free.
It is an act of your will to do so.
You will no longer be chained to the past, but a bright future is in front of you, with Me at the helm.
By you allowing Me to be at the helm, My Light will shine to show you the way that you should go.
Never look back, but always looking ahead and walking on the path that leads to your final destiny.

Colossians 3:13

Forbearing one another, and forgiving one another; if any man have a quarrel against any; even as Christ forgave you, so also do ye.

DAILY ENCOURAGING WORDS...*TO LIVE BY*

July 18th

Arise and shine for the Glory Light of Jesus has come!
Stand, stand firm on My written Word.
As you have a map to guide you, when you need direction,
so it is the same with My written Word and your life.
When you are stuck and do not know which way to turn, that
is when you need My map, which is My written Word.
It will put you on the right path for your life.
It has all the answers to your problems in your life.
When you are sad and overwhelmed, My Word will give you
joy for your sadness, and peace to overcome your
overwhelming feeling.
Read My Word and put it deep into your spirit, that is
where the power is.
The Holy Spirit works with your spirit, and together
releases whatever you need.
Always rely on My Word and My Holy Spirit to lead you
and guide you every moment of your day.
With My Word, you will never be lost or confused.

2nd Samuel 22:31

As for God, His way is perfect, the Word of the Lord is
tried; He is a buckler to all them that trust in Him.

365 Day Devotional...God still speaks today...John 10:27

DAILY ENCOURAGING WORDS...*TO LIVE BY*

July 19th

Arise and shine for the Glory light of Jesus has come!
Walk in the goodness of your God.
Let go and let Me have My way in you.
Open your life and give all to Me.
I AM waiting on you to surrender all to Me.
I AM the God of all.
To be what I have already destined for your life; you only need to surrender all to Me.
There cannot be any flesh operating in you, for while the flesh tries to reign, the Spirit cannot.
This life is a Spirit filled life that must reign in you for you to become the person that I have already planned for you before the foundation of this world.
I have already picked you.
You did not choose Me.

Ephesians 1:4
According as He hath chosen us in Him, before the foundation of the world, that we should be Holy and without blame before Him in Love.

DAILY ENCOURAGING WORDS...*TO LIVE BY*

July 20th

Arise and shine for the Glory Light of Jesus has come!
Be not dismayed, for I AM with you.
I AM working in your life to change what is needed to bring you to the place of maturity in Me.
Keep surrendering your life to Me.
I AM the only one that knows your heart and I can be the only One to change you if you are willing.
All things work together for good for I AM good, and I see the potential in you and the willingness to have Me, do the work in you.
Then and only then, you will be able to do the works that I have called you to do, I can only go as far as you will let Me.
I long to see you go all the way.
Allow Me to work in you, we can achieve this goal together.
Put your faith in Me and worship and praise Me.
Let nothing else pass your lips.
I am moved by the praises of My children.
That is where the power is, and by faith.
All things are done by Faith in Me and the work of the Cross.

Deuteronomy 31:8

And the Lord, Himself goes before thee; He will be with thee, He will not fail thee, neither forsake thee; fear not, neither be dismayed.

DAILY ENCOURAGING WORDS...*TO LIVE BY*

July 21st

Arise and shine for the Glory Light of Jesus has come.
In this day you will see the Hand of God move in your life.
So, keep your heart and mind open so that you will not miss what I have for you.
Always be in a place of receiving and giving praise unto Me.
As you stay in that place of worship, you will be open to whatever I AM doing in your life.
You see it is your faith and worship unto Me that activates My Hand in your life.
When you praise Me, I see where you heart is, it is wide open towards Me.
You can live in that atmosphere all the time.
You live it in your spirit.
Your spirit becomes so strong, it will override your soul and Mine.
This is where I long for My children to live out their lives unto Me.

Psalm 112:1
Praise ye the Lord. Blessed is the man that feareth the Lord, that delighteth greatly in His commandments.

DAILY ENCOURAGING WORDS...*TO LIVE BY*

July 22nd

Arise and shine for the Glory Light of Jesus has come!
This is the way, walk ye in it.
It has already been laid out for you.
Everything has been put into place.
You even have a Guide to help you on your way, and this Guide is the Holy Spirit.
He is waiting on you to ask for His help in anything that has come against you.
When you come to a crossroad in your life and you cannot seem to work out which way to go, the Holy Spirit will direct you, if you only would ask Him.
He has all the answers.
If you try to do it on your own, you will make the wrong choice and that will take you off your pathway.
But with the Holy Spirit working with you, all will be well.
He is the Power, trust Him and you will never fail.

1st Corinthians 3:16
Know ye not that ye are the Temple of God, and that the Spirit of God dwelleth in you?

365 Day Devotional...God still speaks today...John 10:27

DAILY ENCOURAGING WORDS...*TO LIVE BY*

July 23rd

Arise and shine for the Glory light of Jesus has come!
Do you not see how My hand has been moving in your life?
I long to bring you to a place where you will walk in victory everyday.
It is possible to do this very thing, for you have My Holy Spirit living in you and He will help you daily.
Your part is to surrender everything that would hold you back from walking in complete victory.
It is your choice that you will walk out of defeat and into a life of walking in My Love, Joy, and Peace.
Satan cannot stand to be around you when you walk in My attributes.
These attributes become a weapon against Satan.
Nothing will hinder your walk if you stay in the realm of My Holy Spirit.
You will always overcome.

1st Corinthians 15:57
But thanks be to God, which giveth us the victory through our Lord Jesus Christ.

DAILY ENCOURAGING WORDS...*TO LIVE BY*

July 24th
Arise and shine for the Glory Light of Jesus has come!
Trust in Me this day, for I Am in it.
Know that you have all the power and strength from your
God to go through anything that comes your way today.
Look to Me for everything.
I AM not just in one part of your life, but I AM is interested
in every part of your life.
You are made in the image of Me, so you are part of Me.
You have the DNA of Me in you.
That is why I call you to a higher lifestyle than what the
world has.
You walk in My light, not in the darkness of this world.
Keep your eyes on Me and don't listen to the voices that
would try to tell you otherwise.
I AM the way the truth and the life.

John 8:12
Then spake Jesus again unto them saying; I Am the light of
the world; he that followeth Me shall not walk in darkness
but shall have the Light of life.

365 Day Devotional...God still speaks today...John 10:27

July 25th

Arise and shine for the Glory Light of Jesus has come!
Be still and know that I AM your God.
I have seen the activity that has taken place in your life.
Just surrender all to Me, My child and know that I will take care of all things.
Keep your eyes on Me and do not give into these activities of the world.
Draw your strength from Me.
When you think all is lost, know that all is not lost My child.
I have the situation in My Hands and know that I will work things out for you.
I will cause good to come out of all this.
Trust Me, praise Me and lean on Me.
There is nothing that you can do.
Do not let issues of the world continue to wear you down.
Put all under My Blood and know that all is well.

Psalm 105:4
Seek the Lord, and His strength; seek His face evermore.

DAILY ENCOURAGING WORDS...*TO LIVE BY*

July 26th

Arise and shine for the Glory Light of Jesus has come!
Draw nigh to Me and I will draw nigh unto you.
Search for Me and you will find Me.
I AM close to you, as your own breath, for I live within you.
Look deep within and you will find all that you need.
That is where My Love, Joy and Peace reside.
These are crucial to your walk every minute of your day.
With these three working in you and through you, it will keep Satan from bothering you.
He cannot stand the Love, Joy, and Peace that flows through you.
They are weapons to use against Him.
They are also powerful for your life to explode in Me.
The people around you will see and feel the power of these three working in your life.
They will see Jesus in you, and it will lead them to want what you have, and you can tell them that this is from your Lord and Savior, Jesus Christ.

Romans 5:13
Now the God of Hope fill you with all joy and peace in believing that ye may abound in Hope, through the power of the Holy Spirit.

365 Day Devotional...God still speaks today...John 10:27

DAILY ENCOURAGING WORDS...*TO LIVE BY*

July 27th

Arise and shine for the Glory light of Jesus has come!
Arise and sit by My side.
I long to fellowship with you.
Cast all your care on Me, for I care for you.
I long to see you step out and put your trust in Me.
Look beyond your circumstance and see that I will move upon them and turn them around for the good.
When you keep your eyes on Me and not on the things around you, you will know that I Am the only way out for you.
I AM the Light in a dark world.
I see way beyond the situation and have the answers for you.
There is nothing to hard for Me.
I can do the impossible.
So, I say surrender all to Me and trust and believe and receive from My Hand.
I will never leave you nor forsake you.

1st Peter 5:7
Casting all your care upon Him; for He careth for you.

365 Day Devotional...God still speaks today...John 10:27

July 28th

Arise and shine for the Glory Light of Jesus has come!
Let Me lead you, do not lean unto your own understanding.
When you get over into the natural mind, you turn from Me and the Spirit realm.
This is where I want you to live out your life.
You cannot live for Me, if you live in the natural realm for, they do not work together, but they work against each other.
So, you cannot move, but you are stuck and do not have freedom to do anything.
It is like going around and around and going nowhere.
I tell you to renew your mind and get it lined up with My Word, so that you can get back on track.
Renew your faith in Me by putting My Word into your spirit.
Faith cometh by hearing the Word.
Stand upon My Word, for it will never fail you.
Come to Me and I will help you.
Lean on Me.

Romans 10:17
So, then faith cometh by hearing, and hearing by the Word of God.

DAILY ENCOURAGING WORDS...*TO LIVE BY*

July 29th

Arise shine for the Glory Light of Jesus has come!
Do not fret My child, for I AM with thee.
Settle your mind and let go of all the things that have been holding you back from Me and have been stopping you from depending on Me for all.
There is no situation that I cannot handle for good will come out of it.
I AM, able to turn things around from bad to good.
You cannot do this for you do not see the whole picture but only in part.
So, stop trying to do My job.
All I AM asking from you, is to praise Me and believe and know that I AM is working out the problems.
Stand in faith and all is well.
Keep your eyes on Me and be not distracted by anything of this world.

Psalm 46:1
God is our refuge and strength, and ever-present help in trouble.

DAILY ENCOURAGING WORDS...*TO LIVE BY*

July 30th

Arise and shine for the Glory Light of Jesus has come!
Take My Hand it is outstretched to you.
I AM always waiting on you to realize that I AM truly wanting to help you through your day.
When you think that all is lost and you see no hope, that is the time to come to Me and give all to Me.
By doing this, then an only then can I work on your behalf.
I want you to trust Me with your life to turn it completely over to Me.
When you do this, then you will know that all is well in My Hands.
Don't let anything hinder you from doing this.
Keep your eyes on Me and praise Me with all your heart.
When you do this, you will see the change in your life for the better.
You will have peace and joy operate in your life and it will sustain you through your day.
Learn to live in the realm of the Holy Spirit which lives in you.

Psalm 37:5

Commit thy way unto the Lord, trust also in Him and He shall bring it to pass.

DAILY ENCOURAGING WORDS...*TO LIVE BY*

July 31st

Arise and shine for the Glory Light of Jesus has come!
Have I not said unto you, let go of things that would hold you back from what I want to do for you?
You are the only one that can stop My Hand from blessing you.
There is nothing in this world that would be worth leaving your belief in Me.
Satan is a great deceiver; you need to spend time with Me in My Word to gain great discernment.
These are the things that will keep you on track and keeps Satan from stealing your blessings from Me.
It is an ongoing battle, day by day.
Learn to put time aside just for Me.
If you do this, you will become stronger in Me and you will be able to handle the onslaughts from the evil one.
Always remember he is your enemy.
Walk in love, and peace will be your mainstay.

Philippians 4:9
Those things, which ye have both learned, and received, and heard and seen in Me, do, and the God of Peace shall be with you.

DAILY ENCOURAGING WORDS...*TO LIVE BY*

AUGUST

John 10:10

The thief comes only to steal and kill and destroy; I came that they may have life, and have it abundantly.

DAILY ENCOURAGING WORDS...*TO LIVE BY*

August 1st

Arise shine for the Glory Light of Jesus has come!
Let Me work in you this day.
Surrender all to Me, your mind, your emotions, and your will.
Let My Holy Spirit have full control of them all, so that He will b able to bring you in line with My Word.
As you surrender your will to the Holy Spirit, He can move and is able to cause your will to come in line with what I want for your life.
You must be willing to let go of the things in your life that would harm you and get you off track for what I want for you.
Surrender your mind to My Spirit so that He can cleanse your mind and then it will line up with what My Word says, and then your emotions will begin to come into place, and you will begin to feel things lining up for Me, within you.
The mind, the emotions and they will then become a life that will honour your Lord and Savior.
surrender all to Me and see the Mighty Hand of your God work in your life.

Galatians 5:16
This I say then, walk in the Spirit, and ye shall not fulfill the lusts of the flesh.

DAILY ENCOURAGING WORDS...*TO LIVE BY*

August 2nd

Arise and shine for the Glory Light of Jesus has come!
Call out to Me, and put your hand in My hand, for I AM here for you.
I reside in you, although many times you feel that I AM not there or that I have forgotten you.
That is not the case, when you feel this way, there has been something happening in your life that clouds your way, and you cannot feel My presence.
When you feel this way, you need to step into faith and override the situation and reach out to Me.
Know that I will never leave you nor forsake you.
This is what the enemy of your soul (Satan) would like to have you think.
He is a liar and a deceiver.
You need to know My written Word, so that you will be able to recognize the ways of your enemy.
Stand strong on My Word and learn to take authority over him and stop him in his tracks.
I have given you the authority, learn to use it in your life so you can walk in victory and live a strong life in Me and for Me.

Romans 8:37

Nay, in all these things we are more than conquerors through Him that loved us.

DAILY ENCOURAGING WORDS...*TO LIVE BY*

August 3rd

Arise and shine for the Glory Light of Jesus has come!
Expect, expect My Hand to move on your behalf this day.
I AM a God of Miracles.
I AM the same yesterday today and forever.
I AM a God that does not lie for I AM truth.
I have never stopped doing miracles,
As you release your faith and believe that I still do miracles today, I do them everyday, and the only way you will see them is to be expecting to see them in your life.
Ask Me for miracles, these things that seem unbearable in your life, and you see no way out.
Ask, believe, and receive.
Keep looking for things to change in your life.
I long to work miracles on your behalf, to see your life change so I can lead you into a life that is full, and that My Joy would override your sadness.
My way is full of Love, Joy, and Peace.
Receive and live in My Love, Joy, and Peace this day.
Keep expecting.

Matthew 7:7
Ask, and it shall be given you; seek, and ye shall find; knock, and it shall be opened unto you.

DAILY ENCOURAGING WORDS...*TO LIVE BY*

August 4th

Arise and shine for the Glory Light of Jesus has come!
Do you not know that I see you and all that you do and think upon?
I hear you when you cry out to Me.
I planned your life even before you were conceived in your mother's womb.
I have written down everyday of your life, that which you should do.
I have provided for all that I have planned for you, so, that you would be able to do what I have called you to do.
I know that you have pulled away and have gone off track with Me.
I love you so that I continue to call to your heart to come back to Me and surrender all to Me and repent for straying from your path that was designed for you.
I love you and I will never let you go.
I will keep calling to you so that you will walk out your life in Me, and all that I have for you.
Praise Me and trust Me as you surrender all to Me.

Jeremiah 29:11

For I know the thoughts that I think toward you, saith the Lord, thoughts of Peace, and not of evil, to give you an expected end.

365 Day Devotional...God still speaks today...John 10:27

DAILY ENCOURAGING WORDS...*TO LIVE BY*

August 5th

Arise and shine for the Glory Light of Jesus has come!
Have I not said that I AM your source?
Every need that you have, give it to Me.
Have I not said put forth your petition and stand believing that you have what you petitioned for, and it will come to pass?
I AM a God of truth, My ears are open to My children.
I hear and I act on your faith to bring all to pass.
I see and know all your needs.
When you ask, do not give up until you see your petition has come forth.
I AM not only interested in your needs, but I want you to go beyond your needs and ask Me for your wants.
Reach beyond yourself and put all before Me.
I AM a God of more than enough.
I want My children to be blessed way beyond their capabilities.
So, fully trust Me to work everything out in your life.
I am the ALL sufficient one.

Philippians 4:19
But My God shall supply all your needs according to His riches in Glory by Christ Jesus.

DAILY ENCOURAGING WORDS...*TO LIVE BY*

August 6th

Arise and shine for the Glory Light of Jesus has come!
Let My Light shine through you this day.
Let the power of the Holy Spirit work in you and through you, I want to take away the impurities of your life that does not Glorify Me.
I AM a pure God, and I am working in your life to bring you to a place of purity in Me.
I AM calling you to live a Holy and pure life for Me so that I can use you to touch and lead others into My Kingdom.
I AM coming soon; I AM coming for My Bride.
Will you allow Me to work in your life so that you will be an honorable vessel for My use?
The people of this world are hurting and wanting a better life and don't know what to do to have that better life.
How will they find the answer?
They will know when they see My people living a pure life and letting the Love, My Love working in and through your life sharing My Love with all people.
The highest calling is walking in My Love.
So let My Love flow out of you this day.

1st *Thessalonians* 3:12

And the Lord make you to increase and abound in love one toward another, and toward all men, even as we do toward You:

DAILY ENCOURAGING WORDS...*TO LIVE BY*

August 7th

Arise and shine for the Glory Light of Jesus has come!
Step out in faith and begin to praise Me.
Just let go and let Me take the reins of your life and I will lead you where I want to take you.
Press into Me and I will give you directions in what you should do for this day.
Trust Me, for I have a special plan for your life.
You do not have to be concerned about any part of your life.
When you walk in My Peace, in knowing that all is well, you will be able to grow more in the things of the Holy Spirit and will be able to walk in the Holy Spirit instead of the flesh.
Remember that the Holy Spirit gives life, but the flesh will hold you back and destroy your walk with Me.
This is a Spiritual walk and a Glorious one.
Eyes have not seen, nor ears have not heard what God hath prepared for them that love Him.
Stay close to Me and praise Me and Honor Me.
Go about your day, you are Blessed!

1st Corinthians 2:9

But as it is written, eye hath not seen, nor ear heard, neither have entered the heart of man, the things which God hath prepared for them that love Him.

365 Day Devotional...God still speaks today...John 10:27

DAILY ENCOURAGING WORDS...*TO LIVE BY*

August 8th

Arise and shine for the Glory Light of Jesus has come!
Do you not know of the goodness that I pour into your life everyday?
I AM your Provider and Healer of your body, mind emotions will and spirituality.
I want all My children to be whole in Me.
As you surrender all your heart, mind, emotions, will and body to Me, I will make you whole.
You cannot walk in the fullness of Me when you are hurting so bad that you cannot see the way before you.
You stumble and fall, you need not stay down when you fall.
Look up to Me and cry out to Me and I will be there to help you up and to put your back on the right path.
When you see the Glory Light, follow Me.
I AM that Light that shows you the way to go in your life.
Once you are on the right course, do not look back, but keep moving forward and trust Me that I AM doing the work in you to make you whole.
I love you, go about your day.

Proverbs 3: 5-6

Trust in the Lord with all your heart and lean not unto thine own understanding. In all your ways acknowledge Him, and He shall direct your path.

DAILY ENCOURAGING WORDS...*TO LIVE BY*

August 9th

Arise and shine for the Glory Light of Jesus has come!
Praise Me, Praise Me.
All good gifts come from Me.
All Grace and Mercy flows from Me this day.
This is a great day of rejoicing, do not miss the opportunities that will come your way this day.
You need to be looking for them.
I will bless you as you take hold of them.
Press into Me and I will show you the way to go.
These are the days to seek My face and press into Me.
Each day as you get closer and closer to Me, you will become stronger in Me, and you will be able to do the things that I have called you to do.
You will be able to walk in faith and you will see great changes in your life.
As you see these changes, you will marvel at the mighty hand of God working on your behalf.
I AM working in your life, more than you know and can see.
I love you and I want to see you excel more and more everyday of your life.

Psalms 5:11

But let all those that put their trust in Thee rejoice, let them ever shout for joy, because Thou defendest them, let them also that love thy name be joyful in thee.

DAILY ENCOURAGING WORDS...*TO LIVE BY*

August 10th

Arise and shine for the Glory Light of Jesus has come!
Look to Me and see the goodness that flows from Me into your life.
As you open to Me and praise Me and honour Me, I will shower you with Blessings that you will not be able to contain, you will be so overwhelmed.
This is the Heart of the Father, to be able to bless His children to overflowing.
This is why your need to live a pure life for Me, to give up all the things that would not let you grow close to Me.
Once you realize that a pure walk with Me, you will enable all the goodness of life and it will begin to flow, not just one day but every day of your life.
You will walk in My Peace, Joy and My Love that is pure and powerful to be able to live the kind of life before Me.
Surrender all to Me and live in the abundance of life that I died to give you.
Remember I will never leave you, nor forsake you.

Joshua 1:5

There shall not any man be able to stand before thee all the days of thy life: as I was with Moses, so I will be with thee: I will not fail thee, nor forsake thee.

365 Day Devotional...God still speaks today...John 10:27

DAILY ENCOURAGING WORDS...*TO LIVE BY*

August 11th
Arise and shine for the Glory Light of Jesus has come!
Be not concerned, but put your trust in Me.
There is nothing too hard or too big for Me to handle.
I go before you and make the crooked way straight.
My Hand is always on you, to guide you and help you to walk out your walk in Me.
Praise Me and let My Peace, Joy and Love come forth within you.
This is the power that will sustain you through all that comes your way.
They will carry you through.
Keep your eyes on Me.
Trust Me and see what I will do for you.
I love you My child and I walk with you daily.
My eyes are on You.
I never take them off from you.
You are in the Palm of My Hand.
So, I say go forth this day and be blessed!

Isaiah 15.2
I will go before thee, and make the crooked places straight, I will break in pieces the gates of brass, and cut in sunder, the bars of iron.

365 Day Devotional...God still speaks today...John 10:27

DAILY ENCOURAGING WORDS...*TO LIVE BY*

August 12th

Arise and shine for the Glory Light of Jesus has come!
I AM with you this day.
All though the winds of adversities are blowing, My Holy Spirit is blowing upon your soul and spirit, to blow away all things in your life that are not of Me, that you will stand pure before Me.
As you call out to Me, I will answer you and in your time of distress, I look upon you and see your heart.
I know that you are open to Me, and I will honor you because of your faithfulness.
Lean not upon your own understanding for it will not guide you in the right way but lean on Me and know that I will guide you in the way you should go.
We will walk hand in hand and will be victorious.
I love you and will never leave you.
My Light shines in you and all around you.
You are Mine and I AM yours.
You are Blessed.

Psalms 32:8
I will instruct thee and teach thee in the way which thou shalt go. I will guide thee with Mine eye.

DAILY ENCOURAGING WORDS...*TO LIVE BY*

August 13th

Arise and shine for the Glory Light of Jesus has come!
Today is the day to see a great change in your life.
Put your trust in Me and allow Me to work in you and through you.
I have seen the longing in your heart to go higher and higher in Me, and to walk with Me to the point where My Glory Light will fill you up to overflow.
To the place where there is no darkness in you at all.
That is the place I AM calling all My children to come to in their lives.
That is where the true life will shine forth and true power to overcome offence an come to the place in your life that no matter what has been done or said to you, it will not hurt you or move you to take that offence.
Just trust Me, and you will come to that place in your life.

Philippians 4:13
I can do all things through Christ which strengtheneth me.

DAILY ENCOURAGING WORDS...*TO LIVE BY*

August 14th

Arise and shine for the Glory Light of Jesus has come!
I have come so that you may have life and have it more abundantly.
I gave My Life on the Cross, so that you would be able to live a life full of power, joy, peace, and love.
You would not have to live in lack, sickness or loneliness or anything that would be negative.
Everything that I died for is available for you this day.
I long to see you living a life full of goodness.
Surrender all to Me that holds you down (sickness, pain, loneliness, lack) and I will turn your life around.
Just come to Me.
Surrender all and take My Love and My ways of living a good and prosperous life.
I long to see My children living in victory and enjoying their life in Me.

John 10:10

The thief cometh not, but for to steal, and to kill, and to destroy, I AM come that they might have life, and that they might have it more abundantly.

365 Day Devotional...God still speaks today...John 10:27

DAILY ENCOURAGING WORDS...*TO LIVE BY*

August 15th

Arise and shine for the Glory Light of Jesus has come!
Come and take My Hand, let us walk together in this day.
I will lead you and show you the way in which you should go.
When we walk together things flow.
It is when you let go of My Hand and you take your eyes off Me, then you get into demise.
Your mind will follow where your eyes go.
You have the power to control what you look at.
You also have the power to rule over your five senses.
You no longer walk after the flesh, when you gave yourself to Me, but you are to always walk in the Holy Spirit.
Put Him first in your life.
He has all the answers to everything.
Be quick to ask Him and He will be quick to answer you.
Never give up for you do not walk alone.
I will never leave you.
You are My child.

Romans 8:6
For to be carnally minded is death, but to be spiritually minded is life and peace.

DAILY ENCOURAGING WORDS...*TO LIVE BY*

August 16th

Arise and shine for the Glory Light of Jesus has come!
Let the Glory Light rap around you like a garment.
It will protect you, for My Glory Light is all that I AM.
All the power and strength come from Me.
There is nothing more you need to walk out your life in.
When you are allowing My Glory Light to work through you and in you, My Light will permeate through you.
People will know who you serve when they see the Light shine from you.
when you live a pure life before Me, this is what happens to you.
When you are clean pure before Me, you allow My Holy Spirit to work in you and the Glory Light can shine in and through you, you will walk in the abundant life that I long for you to have.
Walk with Me this day and be blessed!

Matthew 5:16
Let your light so shine before men, that they see your good works, and Glorify your Father, which is in Heaven.

DAILY ENCOURAGING WORDS...*TO LIVE BY*

August 17th
Arise and shine for the Glory Light of Jesus has come!
Walk in thanksgiving, being thankful for the blessing that I have blessed you with.
The very breath that you breathe comes from Me.
I watch over you with an everlasting love.
I watch over you, My eyes never leave you.
I sing over you with great joy.
I gave up My life so that you could be redeemed and have a rich and full life.
I gave you everything that I have.
You are joint heirs with Me.
I gave you all, will you not give Me your all?
Surrender your life to Me and walk in the fullness of Me.

Ephesians 5:20
Giving thanks always for all things unto God and the Father in the name of our Lord Jesus Christ.

DAILY ENCOURAGING WORDS...*TO LIVE BY*

August 18th

Arise and shine for the Glory Light of Jesus has come!
Look to Me the Author and Finisher of your faith.
As you look to Me, I will show you the way to go.
The way is not in the past nor is it in the future.
The only way is in the now.
If you look to the past, it will keep you in bondage and if you continually look to the future, you will be lost for the future is not here yet and keeps you in bondage.
The present is where I AM.
If you are not living in the now, you will lose out what I have for you now, this day.
That is why I say to look to Me, for I will guide you and keep you on the right path for your life.
Only I can know what the future holds for you.
If you put your faith in Me, know that My plans for you are good and your life will be fulfilled in Me.
So, concentrate on Me, the Author, and Finisher of your Faith.

Hebrews 12:2

Looking unto Jesus the Author and finisher of our faith, who for the joy that was set before Him endured the Cross, despising the shame, and is set down at the right hand of the throne of God.

DAILY ENCOURAGING WORDS...*TO LIVE BY*

August 19th

Arise shine for the Glory Light of Jesus has come.
Come to Me and start your day by telling Me what is on your heart.
When you look at your day and you see such a heavy load and all that needs to be done, you ponder even if you have the strength to do it.
When you come to Me first and talk to Me about your day, I will be able to help you and tell you how you can accomplish all.
As you sit at My Feet you are already getting your strength from Me.
As you ask, I will equip you for the tasks at hand.
Just trust Me and put your life in My Hands, for I will lead you and the burdens will roll off you, upon Me, for I AM your burden bearer.
Praise Me and give Me thanks for all that I do for you.
When you trust Me, all things will fall into place.
Put Me first in your life and see what I will do for you.
Surrender all to Me.

Proverbs 8:17
I love them that love Me, and those that seek Me early shall find Me.

DAILY ENCOURAGING WORDS...*TO LIVE BY*

August 20th

Arise and shine for the Glory Light of Jesus has come!
Take joy in the One who loves you and upholds you in the Palm of His Hand.
Take courage and praise and honor Me today.
As you walk in Me, nothing can touch you.
There is peace, joy, and love always living inside of you.
As you praise Me, you cause the love, joy, and peace to be active inside of you to live for Me.
It is the Holy Spirit inside of you that helps you walk in the journey I have put you on.
A journey that will honor Me and cause you to have a glorious life.
So, trust Me and walk out your life and walk in the power of the Holy Spirit.
Be Blessed this day My Children.

Romans 14:17
"For the kingdom of God is not meat and drink; but Righteousness and Peace, and Joy in the Holy Ghost."

365 Day Devotional...God still speaks today...John 10:27

DAILY ENCOURAGING WORDS...*TO LIVE BY*

August 21st

Arise and shine for the Glory Light of Jesus has come!
Move forth this day in faith.
Looking to Me for all your needs.
Leave all behind and concentrate on My Hand opening upon your situation to bring the goodness forth this day.
Trust in Me and praise Me and let your faith soar.
Leave all fear, doubt, and unbelief behind you, so that there will be nothing stopping My Hand from moving on your behalf.
Faith is your power to bring forth everything you want and need.
It is the only thing that moves my Hand, to bring forth what you ask for.
Do not allow Satan to stop you from using your faith.
Watch what you say and do, your words have power to hinder your faith from coming forth.
He (Satan) does not want you to succeed in any part of your life.
So, be aware of what you say and do, keep on thanking Me and praising Me for what you ask Me for.

Hebrews 11:1

Now faith is the substances of things hoped for, the evidence of things not seen.

DAILY ENCOURAGING WORDS...*TO LIVE BY*

August 22nd

Arise and shine for the Glory Light of Jesus has come!
This is another day, fret not but look to the One who loves you and can see you through everyday.
Put aside everything that upsets you, and you cannot seem to see the end.
Put your trust in Me and give these things to Me.
You need not keep them, for they will bring you down.
I will raise you above all the things that will come against you.
I AM your strength, so press into Me.
Praise Me and give Me Glory and keep your eyes on Me.
Remember you are in the Palm of My Hand.
You will always be safe here.

1st Peter 5:7
Casting all your care upon Him, for He careth for you.

DAILY ENCOURAGING WORDS...*TO LIVE BY*

August 23rd

Arise and shine for the Glory light of Jesus has come!
Fret not My child, you are in My Hands.
I see all that is happening in your life.
It may not be what you have imagined or what you thought it would be but know that I AM always with you.
My Hand is upon your life, and I guide you in the way that you showed go.
I AM working in your life to accomplish what I want to come forth, so that you will be useful for My calling that is in your life.
So, do not let go of Me, and press into Me more and more, as you do this, you will see your life begin to be full of My Joy, and Peace that will sustain you and make you stronger and stronger every day.
Do not look around you but only look to Me.
Keep your eyes on Me, for I AM your source.
There is no another.

Isaiah 26:3
Thou will keep in perfect peace, whose mind is stayed on thee.

DAILY ENCOURAGING WORDS...*TO LIVE BY*

August 24th

Arise and shine for the Glory Light of Jesus has come!
The Joy of the Lord is your strength.
I call you forth this day to walk in My Joy, and Peace.
When you surrender your life to Me, I give you My Peace, and My Joy.
If you will wall in these, there is no way that the devil will be able to stop you from living a full life in Me.
If you watch what comes out of your mouth, remember that life and death is in your tongue.
When you choose to live for Me and walk in My ways, this is life, if you choose to use your mouth for darkness, you will allow the devil to come into your life and he will create all kinds of chaos and all that comes with darkness.
There is no good thing in serving the devil.
So, I AM calling My children to live in My Glory Light, for all good things come from Me.
Surrender to Me and see that I love you and want to see you live in My fullness, all I have is yours.
Receive it now, I give it to you.

Proverbs 18:21
Death and life are in the power of the tongue.

DAILY ENCOURAGING WORDS...*TO LIVE BY*

August 25th

Arise and shine for the Glory Light of Jesus has come!
Step out into faith.
Faith is the key that opens My Hand to move on your behalf.
Without faith, there is nothing that will move Me.
For I AM Spirt and the things that you want are also in the Spirit realm.
Faith works with the Holy Spirit to bring forth what you are asking for.
Faith comes by the hearing of My Word.
My Word begins to work in your spirit and brings forth the faith needed to produce what you have asked for.
So, you see, it is so important to put My written Word into your spirit, so that faith will grow.
Without faith, you cannot grow in Me.
For your whole walk is a faith walk.

Hebrews 11:1
Now faith is the substance of things hoped for, the evidence of things not see.

DAILY ENCOURAGING WORDS...*TO LIVE BY*

August 26th

Arise and shine for the Glory Light of Jesus has come!
I AM is in this beautiful day.
I have created this day for My creation to enjoy and walk in the Goodness of Me, the Creator.
I love My creation.
I died for all.
No one is left out.
I laid down My Life and rose from the dead so that all mankind could have life and live with Me for all eternity.
The Blood I shed on the Cross paid for the sins of the world.
Come to Me and receive Me.
Call upon My Name and I will answer you and receive you.
I Love you with an everlasting love.
There is no other way to Heaven but by Me.
Go about your day and walk in Me.

John 3:16
For God so Loved the world, that He gave His only begotten Son, that whosoever believeth in Him should not perish, but have everlasting life.

DAILY ENCOURAGING WORDS...*TO LIVE BY*

August 27th

Arise and shine for the Glory Light of Jesus has come!
Lift your head to the One that looks upon you.
My eyes are always looking over you.
Know that you are always on My Mind.
There is not a minute that goes by, that I AM looking for a way to bless you.
This is why you need to be aware and call upon My Name in prayer and in faith believing that I hear you and will answer your petition that you have put before Me.
Do not ask amiss.
Let your prayers come from your heart and not out of selfish motives.
Look beyond yourself and reach out to others that are in want.
When you do this, then I see that you are putting other people first instead of putting yourself first.
In doing this, I see that I can bless you and that is My desire for all My children.

1st Peter 3:12
For the Eyes of the Lord are over the righteous, and His Ears are open into their prayers, but the Face of the Lord is against them that do evil.

365 Day Devotional...God still speaks today...John 10:27

DAILY ENCOURAGING WORDS...*TO LIVE BY*

August 28th

Arise and shine for the Glory Light of Jesus has come!
This is the day that the Lord has made, follow Me.
Look to Me, enquire of Me the things that are on your mind.
There is nothing that I cannot do for you.
You need not try to work out things by yourself.
I AM just waiting on you to ask and believe in Me to answer you and give you direction in your every situation.
I know everything about you, I created you and long to give you a good life and see you overcome in all situations.
Lean on Me and praise Me and trust Me.
I AM your strength.
Rely on Me, for I AM there for you always.

Proverbs 3:5
Trust in the Lord with all thine heart and lean not unto thine own understanding.

DAILY ENCOURAGING WORDS...*TO LIVE BY*

August 29th

Arise and shine for the Glory Light of Jesus has come!
In this day you will see the Hand of God move in your life.
So, keep your heart and mind open so that you will not miss what I have for you.
Always be in a place of receiving and giving praise unto Me.
As you stay in that place of worship, you will be open to whatever I AM doing in your life.
You see it is your faith and worship unto Me that activates My Hand in your life.
When you praise Me, I see where your heart is, it is wide open towards Me.
You can lie in that atmosphere all the time.
You live it in your spirit.
Your spirit becomes strong, it will override your soul and mind.
That is where I long for My children to live out their lives unto Me.

Philippians 1;13
I can do all things through Christ who strengthens Me.

DAILY ENCOURAGING WORDS...*TO LIVE BY*

August 30th
Arise and shine for the Glory Light of Jesus has come!
Look unto Me My child and know that you are always on My Mind.
My thoughts and My Eyes are on you continually.
I see and know your heart.
This day walk in My Love, Joy, and Peace, and My Strength.
Commit your ways unto Me and see the Hand of your God move upon your day.
There is nothing impossible for Me, trust in Me and surrender all to Me and know that you are in the Palm of My Hand.
You are My Beloved.
You are Mine and I AM yours.
We will walk Hand in hand throughout your journey in Me.

Psalm 37:5
Commit thy way into the Lord; trust also in Him; and He shall bring it to pass.

365 Day Devotional...God still speaks today...John 10:27

DAILY ENCOURAGING WORDS...*TO LIVE BY*

August 31st

Arise and shine for the Glory Light of Jesus has come!
As the sun shines in a new day, so shines My Glory Light upon you, not just one day but every day.
So, look to Me and receive what I have for you this day.
There is nothing I cannot do for you if you ask in faith and believe in your heart that you shall have what you asked for.
I long to give you your hearts desire.
Empty your mind and your heart of anything that is not of Me and begin to praise and honour Me and see how things will change for you.
Without faith you cannot please Me.
Lean on Me and learn of Me.
This walk is a walk of faith.
When you received Me in Salvation, it was all by FAITH!
When you received the Gift of the Holy Spirit you received this Gift by FAITH!
Everything you do is in Me or for Me, is all done by FAITH.
You need not fear for I AM is with you.
Do not walk in fear but walk by FAITH.

Hebrews 11:6

But without faith it is impossible to please Him, for he that cometh to God must believe that He is, and that He is a rewarder of them that diligently seek Him.

365 Day Devotional...God still speaks today...John 10:27

DAILY ENCOURAGING WORDS...*TO LIVE BY*

SEPTEMBER

Jude 1:2

May mercy and peace and love be multiplied to you.

DAILY ENCOURAGING WORDS...*TO LIVE BY*

September 1st

Arise and shine for the Glory Light of Jesus has come!
When you have surrendered your life completely over to Me, you will find that it is no longer your life but that you have past from darkness into My marvelous Light.
Everything changes and you will see that it is truly a new way of living.
You no longer want to live for just yourself, but I have opened your heart to reach out to others that are hurting.
You will be able to tell them what took place in you when you gave your heart and life to Me.
Continue to surrender all to Me and you will grow and come closer to Me.
The more you seek My Face and put My Word in you, you will be living in whole obedience to Me, walking out your life in the goodness that I have for you.
Always reach higher and desire the way of your Lord and Savior.

2nd Corinthians 5:17
Therefore, if any man (be) in Christ, (he is) a new creature; old things are passed away, behold, all things become new.

September 2nd

Arise and shine for the Glory Light of Jesus has come!
Come and sit with Me for awhile and learn of Me.
Take time within your day to be able to talk to Me, with a clear mind and heart that is open for fellowship with Me.
Nothing is more important for you than to set time aside only for you and Me.
Things in this world in chaos.
You cannot survive without the help of the Holy Spirit.
He is a PERSON, the third part of the Trinity, who lives within you.
He is your helper, and you need to cultivate a person-to-person relationship with Him.
When you become a friend with Him, you will be able to talk to Him and be able to tell Him all that is going on in your life.
He is reliable and will never leave you nor forsake you.
He is always open to you.
So, begin this day to step out and trust Him.

1st Corinthians 6:19

What? Know ye not that your body is the temple of the Holy Ghost (which is) in you, which ye have of God, and ye are not your own?

DAILY ENCOURAGING WORDS...*TO LIVE BY*

September 3rd

Arise and shine for the Glory Light of Jesus has come!
You live in a fallen world My child.
That is why it is so important to come to Me and spend time in My presence to be filled up and over-flowing with My Power to sustain you through your day.
Obstacles will be put in your path, by the evil one, and you must overcome them.
The only way to do this is through My Holy Spirit shewing you the way.
Do not be afraid of what is before you but go in My Strength and Power and you will see that My Hand is going before you, making the crooked way straight.
Trust Me, for I see all things and you are forever in My site.
I already knew what will happen for I set your path in motion.
Remember to set your eyes on Me and not on the world ways.
I will never fail you.

Psalms 27:1
The Lord is my Light and My Salvation, whom shall I fear?
The Lord is the Strength of my life, of whom shall I be afraid:

DAILY ENCOURAGING WORDS...*TO LIVE BY*

September 4th

Arise and shine for the Glory Light of Jesus has come!
My child, I long to take you higher and higher in Me.
As you give Me more and more of yourself to Me.
I will be able to take you higher in Me.
Take captive of your thoughts and anything that is not upright and encouraging.
Cast it down and put it under My Blood.
You must be always on guard of what is captive in your mind.
This is the battle ground for Satan to try and overcome you, to pull you down.
If you do not take captive of your thoughts right away, the thoughts take root and will start to bring you into depression and once this starts, you really must fight to get into right thinking again.
Depression is not of Me.
Learn who you are in Me and who I AM in you.
My Word will set you free and My Word will keep you free.
Speak My Word and walk in My Righteousness and see how fast I will take you higher in Me.

Proverbs 21:23
Whose keepth his mouth and his tongue, keepth his soul from trouble.

DAILY ENCOURAGING WORDS...*TO LIVE BY*

September 5th

Arise and shine for the Glory Light of Jesus has come!

I AM the Light that shineth in a dark place.

The darkness has overtaken the heart of man, but it does not have to be this way.

There is a way that man can overcome darkness in his soul.

That is the Light of My Glory that will set mankind free if he would come to the cross of Calvary; where I died and I rose again unto life and now sit at the Right Hand of My Father.

I took all of mankind's sins on My body so that they could be free and be made whole for all eternity.

Just for receiving what I have done on the Cross.

This will save your soul and change you from what you are now to what I have for you.

I have a good plan for your life.

A life of Abundance and Joy unspeakable.

Come to Me this day and do not delay.

I AM waiting for you.

Ephesians 2:8

For by grace are ye saved through faith, and that not of yourselves (it is) the gift of God.

DAILY ENCOURAGING WORDS...*TO LIVE BY*

September 6th

Arise shine for the Glory Light of Jesus has come!
Although you see the darkness all around you, you need not fear, for you live in My Light and no darkness can stand in My Glory Light.
You need not put up with darkness around you, for I have given you all the power over the darkness.
So, push back the darkness and call forth My Glory Light to shine over you and around you.
You already have the Glory Light in you, so begin to activate it.
Be sure not to engage in any darkness, for if you allow it in your life, it will prevent the power in you to push back the darkness.
Be careful what you look at and what you hear.
It is crucial to heed to My Words, My children.
You are equipped to fight the good fight of faith, so, rise up My children and do so.
This is a new day, so start today.
Rely on the Holy Spirit to walk with you and teach you.

Colossians 2:10
And ye are complete in Him, which is the head of all principality and power.

DAILY ENCOURAGING WORDS...*TO LIVE BY*

September 7th

Arise and shine for the Glory Light of Jesus has come!
See that you walk in Love today, so that all that I want to do in your life is not stopped by letting yourself get into strife and pull you out of love and faith.
Faith worketh by Love, so if the enemy of your soul can interfere with this, he will do so.
It is your part to stay out of strife and surrender all to Me.
We work together, so that you will be able to live the life I have for you, so that you will walk out your destiny.
It does not just fall on you, so be aware in everything you do in your life, that it will be uplifting and bring you closer to Me.
You cannot allow the things of the world to side track you from looking to Me, for I AM the only way.
You need My Supernatural strength to walk in this spiritual life that you are called to walk.
Outside of Me is only heartaches and darkness that will overtake you completely.
Therefore, choose to walk in faith and love which will carry you all the way to the end.

2nd Corinthians 5:7
(For we walk by faith, not by sight).

365 Day Devotional...God still speaks today...John 10:27

DAILY ENCOURAGING WORDS...*TO LIVE BY*

September 8th

Arise and shine for the Glory Light of Jesus has come!
Surrender to Me this day, your life, your desires, your dreams, your expectations and leave nothing out.
I AM the God of the heart.
You see that I have knit you together and placed you into your mother's womb.
There is nothing that you can hide from Me, for you are an open book to Me.
I have even the things you would do and say for everyday written in My Book, for each day of your life.
I know the ups and downs of your life, so, does it not make good sense that you would bring everything to Me?
Ask for My help and strength to go through the days of your life, knowing that I have the Power to take you through successfully each day.
Do not let anyone or anything get in your way of walking out your life in Me and for Me.
Keep your eyes on Me and always trust what I have said.
You are blessed this day.

Psalm 37:5
Commit thy way unto the Lord: trust also in Him, and He shall bring (it) to pass.

365 Day Devotional...God still speaks today...John 10:27

DAILY ENCOURAGING WORDS...*TO LIVE BY*

September 9th

Arise and shine for the Glory light of Jesus has come!
This is the day of rejoicing, to open to your God and realize that I AM always for you and not against you.
There is nothing that could make your God keep the very things that I died for, from blessing you.
My Love for you is everlasting to everlasting.
Do not let Satan take away your blessing that I have given you.
He can attack your mind to try to stop My Hand from working in your life.
You are the only one that can stop the thoughts that come through your mind.
Always be aware of this and stop it before it takes hold of your mind and causes fear, to which fear opens all kinds of things to come into your life.
So, stop him before that can take place in you.
Keep your mind on Me, that way he has no place to bring you down.

Jeremiah 29:11
For I know the thoughts that I think toward you, saith the Lord, thoughts of Peace, and not of evil, to give you an expected end.

365 Day Devotional...God still speaks today...John 10:27

DAILY ENCOURAGING WORDS...*TO LIVE BY*

September 10th

Arise and shine for the Glory Light of Jesus has come!
Be still in your thoughts and know that I AM God.
Take captive of your thoughts for that is the place where the great battles are won.
Keep your mind clear of thoughts that would hinder your life from going forth in a positive way for Me.
Satan will always be trying to take control of your mind.
You have the power and authority in My Name to come against the evil one.
Be always aware, what enters your mind.
If it is a negative thought, you know that it is straight from Satan, so you can come against it and be rid of it.
Put it under My Blood, put your mind in a state of praise and worship unto Me.
Do not listen to anything unclean for it does not honour Me.
Keep your mind clear so that you will be able to hear My voice for I have much to reveal to you.

Romans 12:2

And be not conformed to this world but be ye transformed by the renewing of our mind, that ye may prove what (is) that good, and acceptable and perfect will of God.

September 11th

Arise and shine for the Glory Light of Jesus has come!
Watch and see the Goodness of your God work in your life this day.
As you walk close to Me and depend on the leading of My Holy Spirit, you will be Blessed.
I AM calling My children to walk in the fulness of My Blessing.
Let My Holy Spirit work with you to remove all the hurts and wounds that are in your soul.
Learn to let go of offences and walk in love with all people.
As you ask the Holy Spirit to work with you to be healed in your mind, emotions and in your will, you will both embark on a journey together for this healing to manifest.
When we are whole in our soul, the Lord can use us to carry out the work that each one is called to do.
It is effortless when you allow the Holy Spirit to work with you.
Rely on and expect the Holy Spirit to lead you each day.

3 John 1:2

Beloved, I wish above all things that thou mayest prosper and be in health, even as thy soul prospereth.

DAILY ENCOURAGING WORDS...*TO LIVE BY*

September 12th

Arise and shine for the Glory Light of Jesus has come!
Come and see the beauty of your God.
I AM arrayed in righteousness and truth and My compassion burns in My heart for you.
I see and understand what you are going through.
I say look to Me, and you will see My faithfulness.
I AM far above all circumstances that would arise in your life.
You sit in Heavenly place with Me in Heaven.
My Glory Light flows into you and down into your spirit to give you the answers that you are needing for your circumstances.
So, always look above and expect Me to do the work that needs to be done on your behalf.
There is no need to look to another source, for there is no other way but through Me.
If you center your faith on Me and release that faith, you will have your answer, for I always surrender to faith.
It is what moves Me to work on your behalf.

Ephesians 2:6
And raised us up together and made us sit in Heavenly Places in Christ Jesus.

DAILY ENCOURAGING WORDS...*TO LIVE BY*

September 13th

Arise and shine for the Glory Light of Jesus has come!
Walk in My righteousness, for I have made you righteous, because of the sacrifice that I did for all at Calvary.
You already stand and wear the robe of righteousness.
My Blood paid for it all.
When My Father looks upon His children, He sees nothing but the Blood that was shed by His Son for you.
You are already made righteous before Him.
Choose to walk in righteousness or you will walk in the flesh.
The flesh is nothing but a way of life to satisfy your own longings and makes no way for the Spiritual life.
The righteousness of God will cause you to live your life in doing the things that will satisfy both the Spiritual side in your mind, your emotions, and your will.
You then will be able to make good choices in everything that pertains to every part of your life.
Wear this Robe of righteousness every day of your life.
Believe and receive what I did for you on the Cross, walk in faith and trust Me to carry out all what I said I would do for you.

Psalm 34:15
The eyes of the Lord are upon the righteous, and His ears are open unto their cries.

365 Day Devotional...God still speaks today...John 10:27

DAILY ENCOURAGING WORDS...*TO LIVE BY*

September 14th

Arise and shine for the Glory Light of Jesus has come!
Old things are passed away and behold all things become new.
Each day is new, I never carry over anything from the day before.
If I did this, I would be going against My Word.
I cannot go against My Word, for My Word stands true and will last forever.
So, My child you need to leave behind yesterday and go forward into this brand new day, where all things are new.
Trust Me all the way, for I know the way and what I have promised you I will do.
Stand on this promise, in faith believing in My promise to be done.
No matter what happens, stand firm and speak My Word and decree and declare the outcome.

Job 22:28

Thou shalt also decree a thing, and it shall be established unto thee and the Light shall shine upon thy ways.

DAILY ENCOURAGING WORDS...*TO LIVE BY*

September 15th
Arise and shine for the Glory Light of Jesus has come!
This is a great day My child, for I AM with you.
Everything that I have is yours for the asking and releasing your faith by receiving what you have asked for.
I AM always waiting on My children to come unto Me.
I long just to Bless you.
My Word is full of promises for every part of your life.
These are not released until you ask and stand on the promise and take it for yourself by releasing your faith and know that you shall have it.
You have not for you ask not.
We work together so that all will be fulfilled.
So, do not stay in your lack, when all is provided for you.
I AM merciful and loving that is why I long to set all My children free from lack to see them operating in the fullness that I have for them.

Philippians 4:19
But my God shall supply all your need according to His riches in Glory by Christ Jesus.

DAILY ENCOURAGING WORDS...*TO LIVE BY*

September 16th

Arise and shine for the Glory Light of Jesus has come!
Surrender your thoughts to Me and let your mind be stayed on Me.
Keep your mind clear of things that have no value and will draw you away from Me.
Your mind is a powerful part of you.
If you are not aware of what is going through your mind, you will be led captive of the thoughts that are in your mind.
If they are not good thoughts, they will lead you to become downcast and you will lose your joy that I have put within you.
Always be mindful of every thought that enters your mind.
Do not let the enemy of your soul take over your mind but let the Holy Spirit help you to keep your mind clear of the thoughts that would stop the flow of your joy in your life.
The Joy of the Lord is your strength.
Remember that it is the mind that is the battlefield.
You must learn to keep your mind clear and centered on Me.

Isaiah 26:3
Thou will keep him in perfect peace, whose mind is stayed on Thee, because he trusted in Thee.

DAILY ENCOURAGING WORDS...*TO LIVE BY*

September 17th

Arise and shine for the Glory Light of Jesus has come!
My child, you need not be concerned about what you are faced with, for I AM with you, and I see what is needed at this point in your life.
Continue to look to Me and putting your faith in Me.
I AM working on the areas of your life that needs a door to open for you.
Remember that I AM the door opener and the door closer.
My child I AM about to open a door that will never be closed.
I AM fulfilling what I have put in place at the very beginning of your journey.
If you allow Me to work in you, so that you will be ready to walkout My plans for your life.
By doing so, you will have My perfect Peace, and Joy.
There is total fulfillment in Me, there is no other way.
Never lose hope, hope always in Me, for I will lead you and walk with you all the way to the very end of your journey here on earth.

Psalm 37:5

Commit thy way unto the Lord; trust also in Him, and He shall bring it to pass.

DAILY ENCOURAGING WORDS...*TO LIVE BY*

September 18th

Arise and shine for the Glory Light of Jesus has come!
Come to Me My child when you are weary.
Come to Me when you think that all is gone.
Come to Me when you are ill.
Come to Me when you think no one cares.
Come to Me when things look like all is lost and you are alone.
Come to Me when you are lonely.
Come to Me when you see no way out.
Come to Me when you are stressed to the limit.
Come to Me at last when you have lost all hope, and you are so downcast that you feel the light has gone out.
I have not left you alone.
Look up My child and call on Me.
I AM waiting on you.
Call upon My Name for I will pick you up and place you on the path of hope and place you back where you need to be, for I will never leave you nor forsake you.
Just call out My Name.

Jeremiah 29:11
For I know the thoughts I think toward you saith the Lord, thoughts of peace, and not of evil, to give you an expected end.

September 19th

Arise and shine for the Glory Light of Jesus has come!
Be not dismayed, for I AM with you.
I AM here in the rough times as well as the good times.
Step out in faith and speak forth My Word so that the power of My Word and My Holy Spirit will come forth and begin to work in your situation.
Do not lose sight of the fact that My Hand is always working in your life.
When you feel that all is lost, just surrender all to Me and lean on Me for I will bring you through.
You are strong in Me, and you have My Holy Spirit to lead you through.
He is all wisdom; He is your helper.
Put your trust in Me and look to no man for they are weak.
So, lift your head and know that I AM working on your life and will supply everything that you need.
Go forth and continue to seek My Face and praise Me with all that is within you.
I AM your strength so walk in Me, knowing all is well.

Psalm 46:1
God is our refuge and strength, a very present help in trouble.

DAILY ENCOURAGING WORDS...*TO LIVE BY*

September 20th

Arise and shine for the Glory Light of Jesus has come!
Call upon the Lord, call upon His name.
My name is all powerful.
There is no other name above My Name.
Whatever you ask in the name of Jesus, believing by faith, then it will be done for you.
When you ask and it comes in line with My Will and My Word, it will be done.
My name is above all sickness, all sickness must bow to the name of Jesus.
All poverty must bow to the name of Jesus.
Everything that is of Satan, the enemy of your soul, must bow to the name of Jesus.
I died and shed My Blood and took the stripes on My back for all mankind and all darkness that would keep My children from surrendering to Me.
Come to Me and surrender your life completely to Me and believe with all your heart that I did it all at the Cross.
Believe and receive and confess it with your mouth that I AM your Lord and Savior of your life.

Philippians 2:10
That at the name of Jesus every knee should bow, of things in Heaven, and things in earth, and things under the earth.

365 Day Devotional...God still speaks today...John 10:27

September 21st

Arise and shine for the Glory Light of Jesus has come!
Lookup, look up and put your focus on Me.
Do not look at the things of this world but know that I AM not of this world, but I AM the one who knows and understands everything that goes on in your life.
This world is not your home, so therefore do not look to the ways of this world to help you get through your problems.
The world does not have the answers that you need.
You are called to a higher way of living.
You are spiritually born into the Kingdom of God, which makes Heaven your new home.
This is why I said that this world is no longer your home.
This is just a resting place to get you ready for Heaven.
I have prepared a place for you.
Let Me do the work that needs to be done in you.
Trust Me for I AM the Author and Finisher of your faith.
Keep your eyes on Me and trust Me in all things.

John 14:2

In My Father's House are many mansions, if it were not so, I would have told you. I go to prepare a place for you.

DAILY ENCOURAGING WORDS...*TO LIVE BY*

September 22nd

Arise and shine for the Glory Light of Jesus has come!
Come and let us reason together.
I have made the way open so you can come to the throne room before Me, so that you can bare your soul and tell Me all that is a concern for you.
My ears are open, and My Heart is set towards you.
I know you, for I was the One that created you.
You are fearfully and wonderfully made.
I have designed you precisely for a special part in this time of your life.
If you will allow Me to work in you, so that I can bring you fully prepared into your calling.
Unless you surrender all to Me, you will just stumble along not fully satisfied or complete in your life.
You will not be able to walk out your calling that is on your life.
So, call upon Me and I will answer you.

Philippians 1:6
Being confident of this very thing, that He which hath begun a good work in you, will perform (it) until the day of Jesus Christ.

365 Day Devotional...God still speaks today...John 10:27

DAILY ENCOURAGING WORDS...*TO LIVE BY*

September 23rd

Arise and shine for the Glory Light of Jesus has come!
Come into My presence and spend time with Me.
Let My presence saturates your whole being.
I AM is all that you need.
Look to Me and give Me all.
It is not in your power to face and have the answers that you need for all situations in your life, but the power is in and through Me that is able to dismantle all the situations that come your way.
It does not matter what they are.
Stay in My presence and ask of Me and trust Me, you will be able to live for Me, no matter what.
I AM your all sufficient One, there is no other.
Praise Me and walk in faith and know that you are always safe in My presence.
It is possible to be in My presence for I live within you, through My Holy Spirit.

Psalm 34:19

Many are the afflictions of the righteous, but the Lord delivers him out of them all.

DAILY ENCOURAGING WORDS...*TO LIVE BY*

September 24th

Arise and shine for the Glory Light of Jesus has come!
Stay in My presence and rely on Me, for your day.
Also release your day into My Hands and ask for the leading of the Holy Spirit to work in every part of your life.
He is the strength that gives you power to walk out your day.
You yourself do not have the ability to come against the onslaught of the evil one.
Be aware of the one that would come against you and attempt to destroy you and keep you from having all that I have for you.
Praise Me, and always look to Me and ask Me to help you.
Choose to walk in the Holy Spirit every moment of your day.
There is fulfillment in Me.
Trust Me in every decision you nee to make.
I AM always there for you.

Proverbs 3:5-6

Trust in the Lord with all thine heart and lean not unto thine own understanding.
In all thy ways acknowledge Him, and He shall direct thy path.

365 Day Devotional...God still speaks today...John 10:27

DAILY ENCOURAGING WORDS...*TO LIVE BY*

September 25th

Arise and shine for the Glory Light of Jesus has come!
Consider you walk with Me.
I AM calling My children to a higher level in Me.
I want you to come to Me daily, to be closer to Me.
I AM calling for your life to line up with My Word and walk in My ways.
My ways are more than asking Me to be Lord of your life.
Surrender completely to Me and give Me permission to prepare you for the walk of faith that I have set before you.
Give up the things that tie you down and causes you to stay in one place, instead of moving forward.
The things of this world are lust of the flesh, the lust of the eyes, and the pride of life.
This is not My way.
You must lay all these things down and walk in My ways.
Learn My Word and stand on it.
Believe and trust in My power and strength to live one day at a time.

1st John 2:16

For all that is in the world, the lust of the flesh, and the lust of the eyes and the pride of life is not of the Father but is of the world.

DAILY ENCOURAGING WORDS...*TO LIVE BY*

September 26th

Arise and shine for the Glory Light of Jesus has come!
Go forth, for this is a day of rejoicing.
Reach out to Me and see that My Hand is upon you.
I AM working in your life, know all is well.
Keep on trusting Me and walk in My righteousness and praise Me.
Always walk in My ways.
When you center your mind on Me, then you are putting yourself in My care.
I cannot do anything unless you are willing to lay down your life and put all aside for Me.
Let nothing come between you and Me.
Look unto Me and see what I will do this day.
Let your faith come up to Me.
Let your light shine for Me today.
Wherever you go, uplift Me.
Stand firm in Me, for I AM the Truth, the Life, and the Way.
I love you My child and I will never let you go.

1st Thessalonians 3:8
For now, we live, if ye stand fast in the Lord.

365 Day Devotional...God still speaks today...John 10:27

DAILY ENCOURAGING WORDS...*TO LIVE BY*

September 27th

Arise and shine for the Glory Light of Jesus has come!
Cast aside your thoughts and center in on Me.
Cast all your cares upon Me and know that I AM orchestrating all things concerning you.
Have faith in Me and always lean on Me.
I know more about you than you know about yourself.
I have already planned out your life, I have put things in place for you to carry out what I have planned for you.
You need not thing how it will be done, just know that I have already done it.
Believe in Me and take courage that all is well and take one day at a time.
Put your faith in Me and hold onto My hand I will lead you.
Do not worry if you get off track, for I will lead you back on track.
So, let not your heart be troubled but look to Me for all things.
I love you, and I will never let you go.
You are Mine and I AM yours.

Isaiah 4:13
For I the Lord thy God will hold thy right hand saying unto thee, Fear not; I will help thee.

DAILY ENCOURAGING WORDS...*TO LIVE BY*

September 28th

Arise and shine for the Glory Light of Jesus has come!
Come and walk in My Footsteps.
I have already gone before you and prepared the way for you.
Learn of Me and press into Me, take My Hand and I will lead you all the way through.
Sometimes the way is rough and rocky. But have no fear for I AM with you.
I will give you the strength and power to overcome.
Ask for My Wisdom, Knowledge and Understanding, so, that you will be able to choose what is right for you.
Be not quick to make decisions, until you have asked and used the tools, I have given you.
Let My Peace be your guide in all things.
When you do this, you are walking in My Footsteps.
Always be aware what is going on around you, for I AM there to cheer you on.
I love you with an everlasting love.

John 14:27

Peace, I leave with you, My Peace I give unto you; not as the world giveth, give I unto you.
Let not your heart be troubled, neither let it be afraid.

DAILY ENCOURAGING WORDS...*TO LIVE BY*

September 29th

Arise and shine for the Glory Light of Jesus has come!
Move out of your old life and come into the life that I have for you.
When you surrendered your life to Me, you became a new person, old things passed away and all things became new.
There is no room for two lives, give up the old ways and trust Me to show you the new path that I have prepared for you.
I have given you Peace, Joy, and My Love.
My Love is shed abroad in your heart by My Holy Spirit.
You must choose if you will walk in the new life that I designed for you, and when you do this, things will start to line up with Me, and you will see the change in your life.
Let Me lead you and teach you the ways of Me.
Meditate on My Word and plant it deep in your heart, for it is the power and the strength that will carry you through each day.
Remember it is a walk of faith in you working out your own Salvation, one day at a time.

2nd Corinthians 5:17

Therefore, if any man be in Christ, he is a new creature, old things are passed away, behold all things are become new.

DAILY ENCOURAGING WORDS...*TO LIVE BY*

September 30th
Arise and shine for the Glory Light of Jesus has come!
Be still and know that I AM God.
I see what is going on in you.
I know your hearts desire and that your heart is turned toward Me.
I know the struggles that you go through.
Just remember to lean on Me and ask for help in times of need.
I AM always there for you.
I cannot move on your behalf if you do not cast your cares upon Me.
When you do this, then I can move on your behalf, and start to work things out for you.
Take one day at a time and tell Me all that concerns you.
Co-partner with Me and see how things will come together for you.
Know that I do all thing well, you need not fret for you are in My Hands.

Psalm 143:8
Cause me to hear thy loving kindness in the morning for in Thee do I trust, cause me to know the way wherein I should walk for I lift up my soul unto thee.

365 Day Devotional...God still speaks today...John 10:27

DAILY ENCOURAGING WORDS...*TO LIVE BY*

OCTOBER

1st Thessalonians 5:18

In every thing give thanks: for this is the will of God in Christ Jesus concerning you.

DAILY ENCOURAGING WORDS...*TO LIVE BY*

October 1st

Arise and shine for the Glory Light of Jesus has come!
Do you see the goodness of your God around you?
My Blessings are in the sunshine, in My creation, look above, and be aware of the good things that are happening in you and in your family.
Trust in Me for I hold you in the palm of My Hands.
When you feel weary and things of this world seem to overwhelm you, just surrender all to Me.
I AM your strength that you draw from.
Lean on Me for I AM always with you.
Do not lose sight of Me.
I AM all you need.
Ask of Me and know that I will respond to your faith.
Do not waiver but trust Me and praise Me for and in all things.
Give thanksgiving unto Me and let My Peace and Joy, fill your heart.
All is well.

James 1:17
Every good gift and every perfect gift is from above, and comes down from the Father of Lights with whom there is no variations or shadows of turning.

DAILY ENCOURAGING WORDS...*TO LIVE BY*

October 2nd

Arise and shine for the Glory Light of Jesus has come!
Wait on Me, do not go before Me.
Seek My face and listen with your heart to what I will say.
It does not matter what situation you find yourself in, there is always a way out.
Your mind cannot figure out the answer but only through the Word and the Wisdom of God.
So, pursue both the Word of God and His Wisdom.
You will find the right solution to your situation.
Stay close to Me and do not fret about anything that will only stop the flow of My Spirit from working in you to let you know what you should do.
He is waiting on you to ask of Him to show you what to do.
Be careful for nothing but always be thankful and give praise always unto your God.

1st Chronicles 16:11
Seek the Lord and His strength; seek His Face continually!

365 Day Devotional...God still speaks today...John 10:27

DAILY ENCOURAGING WORDS...*TO LIVE BY*

October 3rd

Arise and shine for the Glory Light of Jesus has come!
As the freshness of the snow that is falling upon the ground, it purifies and brings new life.
So, let My Glory Light fall upon you and let it purify you to bring new life within you.
My Glory Light has the power to take all that deadness out of your life.
As you surrender all to Me, My Gory Light will heal and give new life.
As this process is being done, little by little you will change and become the person I have destined you to be.
You are not strong enough to have My Glory Light all at once.
But as you surrender all to Me, I will cleanse you and you will see the fruit to begin to grow in you.
You will see and feel the difference from the old to the new become a new creature in Me.

2nd Corinthians 5:17

Therefore, if any man is in Christ, he is a new creature, old things are passed away, behold all things become new.

DAILY ENCOURAGING WORDS...*TO LIVE BY*

October 4th

Arise and shine for the Glory Light of Jesus has come!
Let Me lead you into all truth for I AM the truth.
Whenever you need to know and understand what is going on in your life, you cannot see all sides of the situation, but I can.
That is why you always need to be aware and come to Me for the whole truth of the matter.
Satan would like to put you off track by telling you that all is well and there is no need to worry, that all will work out for you.
Do not listen to him but put your trust in Me and allow Me to show you what you need to do and then only then you will be able to see clearly and walk out what I have showed you.
Always come to Me first and do not lean to your own understanding and do not listen to other voices.
Just trust and obey in Me.

Proverbs 30:5
Every Word of God is pure, He is a shield unto them that put their trust in Him.

365 Day Devotional...God still speaks today...John 10:27

DAILY ENCOURAGING WORDS...*TO LIVE BY*

October 5th

Arise and shine for the Glory Light of Jesus has come!
Go about your day and be blessed for My hand is heavy upon you.
As the day goes on and opens to you, know that I AM with you, and I go wherever you go.
So, make the right choices, so that you will not open doors for the evil one to come in and lead you astray.
Always be on guard, for the enemy also is looking for a way to deceive you.
Focus on Me and watch what comes out of your mouth.
When you praise Me and honour Me, that is the power that will help in times of need.
That is a weapon against the enemy of your soul.
He cannot stand before the praises that My people give Me.
It is pure and powerful.
So, praise and faith are mightily in putting the devil to flight.
Keep your eyes on Me and your mouth full of praises unto Me.

Psalm 92:1
It is a good thing to give thanks unto the Lord and to sing praises unto thy name.

DAILY ENCOURAGING WORDS...*TO LIVE BY*

October 6th

Arise and shine for the Glory Light of Jesus has come!

My child do not focus beyond this day.

Keep your eyes on Me and center your thoughts on the things of this day and ask for guidance to help you through your day.

Anything beyond today is fruitless.

I created a day at a time so that My children would not be overwhelmed.

Walk in the Spirit and not in the flesh, for the flesh is out to destroy your walk in the Spirit.

You are first Spirit, then soul (mind, will and emotions) and you live in a body.

So, let My Spirit empower you in all that you do.

When you walk in Me, you will walk in My Joy and Peace and most of all, My Love.

When you walk in My Love, you will be fulfilled in every part of your life.

Lift Me and your day will be fulfilled, and I will be honored.

James 1.11

Where as ye know not what (shall be) on the morrow. For what (is) your life? It is even a vapour, that appeareth for a little time, and then vanishied away.

365 Day Devotional...God still speaks today...John 10:27

DAILY ENCOURAGING WORDS...*TO LIVE BY*

October 7th

Arise and shine for the Glory Light of Jesus has come!
There is Power in My Name, in My Word and in My Blood.

My Word is powerful when you put it into your heart and meditate on it, saying it repeatedly until you have it firmly planted in your spirit.

When troubled times come, you will have it in your spirit and the Holy Spirit will bring it forward so that you can speak it forth into the trouble that arises, and the Word will dispel it.

In the Name Jesus, My Name is Power to come against anything that should arise, and My Name will dispel it.

All things must submit to My Name.

When you believe that My Blood was shed for you on the cross, then you can use it to come against all that would revolt against, every situation must bow to the Blood of the Lamb.

Use My Name, My Word and My Blood to overcome the evil one.

Revelation 12:11
And they overcame him (Satan) by the Blood of the Lamb, and by the Word of their testimony, and they loved not their lives unto their death.

DAILY ENCOURAGING WORDS...*TO LIVE BY*

October 8th

Arise and shine for the Glory Light of Jesus has come!
Let Me guide you in the way you should go.
I know the way for I have already planned out your pathway for your life.
Since I know the way, would it not be wise to follow Me and allow Me to show you the way?
I AM always with you, so it is not a journey to which you have to walk alone.
Put your trust in Me and you will reach your goal, and all I have for you.
You will reach your destiny.
In between the start and finish of your walk, is a life of giving up yourself and let My Love shine through you and out to other people.
Always put Me first and you will not have a problem with loving others.
I AM Love and I live in you by My Holy Spirit.
Allow Him to teach you and to mould you into the person that I have destined you to be.

John 15:12

This is My commandment, that ye love one another, as I have loved you.

DAILY ENCOURAGING WORDS...*TO LIVE BY*

October 9th

Arise and shine for the Glory Light of Jesus has come!
Always look to Me and walk in My Spirit, for the walk of your life is in Me and is not in the natural.
The natural mind cannot understand the spiritual.
It is important to understand this.
You put your trust in Me, and I will see that you walk in My ways.
Feed on My Word and lean on Me for the strength that you need daily.
Take My Peace and walk in it.
I have given you all that you need to walk out your life in power and might.
You are Blessed so walk in Me.

Galatians 5:25
If we live in the Spirit, let us also walk in the Spirit.

DAILY ENCOURAGING WORDS...*TO LIVE BY*

October 10th

Arise and shine for the Glory Light of Jesus has come!
I AM calling My children to walk in the fullness of Me, for all things originated from Me.
You have the power and strength within you to walk out the path of life that I have chosen for you.
When you walk in the Spirit, you are walking in Me.
Within you is My Peace, My Joy, and My Love.
You release these by faith and praise unto Me.
When you sing songs of praise and honour unto Me, that power within you starts to work in your life to set you free and stops the enemy of your soul from working in your life.
You have the power of life and death within your tongue.
Speak life into your circumstances.
It is the words you speak that will set you free to live a life of power that will honour Me.
Keep your eyes on Me and walk out your life in My Power and Strength.
I will never leave you nor forsake you.
You are Blessed

Proverbs 18:21
Death and life are in the power of the tongue; and they that love it shall eat the fruit thereof.

October 11th

Arise and shine for the Glory Light of Jesus has come!

As you spend time in My presence, you will find that I AM with you, and you will feel the closeness that you can have always in My presence.

I AM Spirit and the only way that you can touch Me, is by worshipping Me in Spirit and in truth.

I reside in you, so you can fellowship with Me every moment of the day and night.

Learn to activate the closeness of genuine relationship between you and Me.

You cannot grow in Me without spending time in My Word and spending time in My presence.

As you do this, you allow Me to take you to a higher level in Me.

As you allow Me to do this, the things of this world will no longer hold you back and have power over you.

Greater is He that is in you, than he that is in the world.

So, trust Me and believe what I say, for it will bring you great life and fulfillment.

Psalm 145:18

The Lord is nigh unto all them that call upon Him in truth.

DAILY ENCOURAGING WORDS...*TO LIVE BY*

October 12th

Arise and shine for the Glory Light of Jesus has come!

Now is the time to fully surrender every part of your life.

In total surrender, is where you will find peace, and your mind will be in total clarity.

You will be able to make right decisions on things that have to be addressed.

When your mind is in unrest, it is not able to make or even think straight.

It is an attack of the enemy (Satan) to stop you from going ahead in every area of your life.

It is the mind that when operating clearly, will cause your life to come together, so that you will be made whole.

The mind operates and controls every area of your life, for the mind is part of your soul, along with your emotions and your will.

So, you see that total surrender to Me will allow Me to work in your life to come together in the way that I have destined for you.

Trust Me and walk with Me.

James 4:7

Submit yourself therefore to God, resist the devil, and he will flee from you.

DAILY ENCOURAGING WORDS...*TO LIVE BY*

October 13th

Arise and shine for the Glory Light of Jesus has come!
No matter what situation you find yourself in, all you need to do, is know in your heart that I will never leave you nor forsake you.
This is what you center your hope and trust on.
Things may seem dark and impossible but know that the God of your life is all powerful and can do the impossible.
If you keep your faith centered on Me and not on the situation, all will be well.
I will accomplish what need to be done in that situation.
I have My part and you have your part to do to bring forth the answer to any situation.
Remember faith, trust and standing on My Word is your key.
Do not doubt but only believe.

Psalm 112:7
He shall not be afraid of evil tidings; his heart is fixed, trusting in the Lord.

DAILY ENCOURAGING WORDS...*TO LIVE BY*

October 14th

Arise and shine for the Glory Light of Jesus has come!
Now is the time to put all your faith in Me.
Do not waver and ponder on the things that have no meaning to your Spiritual walk.
Your Spiritual walk is the only thing that has eternal value and will last throughout eternity.
The things that are of this world have no spiritual value whatsoever.
This is why I say to surrender all to Me the things of the past and the things of this world that would hold you back from going forward in achieving your Spiritual life in Me.
All that matters is what is done for Me in this world.
So, focus on Me and keep your eyes upon what I have done for you.
Always trust Me and always rely on My Holy Spirit for the help and strength to guide you in all that you do.
You are never alone at any time in your life.
Be Blessed.

Jude 1:24

Now into Him that is able to keep you from falling, and to present (you) faultless before the presence of His Glory, with exceeding joy.

365 Day Devotional...God still speaks today...John 10:27

DAILY ENCOURAGING WORDS...*TO LIVE BY*

October 15th

Arise and shine for the Glory Light of Jesus has come!
Do you not know that My Power is always within you?
I have taken up residency within you and I will always be there, whenever you need Me.
Call upon My help and wisdom that you need to accomplish whatever is happening to you currently.
When you trust in Me and realize what you have within you, you will never have to be the underdog.
You can and should be on top.
Does My Word declare that you are above and not beneath?
Speak forth My Word and it has the Power to become what it is that you have spoken and have need of.
This will work in every part of your life.
It doesn't matter what it is, big or small.
Just release your faith and watch what I will do for you.
I uphold My Word to bring it too past.
If I did not do this, I would be a liar and that I Am not.
Only believe that all things are possible with Me.

Ephesians 1:19
And what is the exceeding greatness of His power to usward who believe, according to the working of His Mighty Power.

365 Day Devotional...God still speaks today...John 10:27

DAILY ENCOURAGING WORDS...*TO LIVE BY*

October 16th

Arise and shine for the Glory Light of Jesus has come!
When you get pulled down under life's trials, do not stay there, but come to Me and surrender all to Me.
Repent and let My Blood wash it all away and it will never be brought to your account again.
It is gone forever.
Trust that My Blood is all powerful to do this.
Forgive yourself and put it to rest.
It cannot hurt you anymore, it is gone.
Do not keep thinking about it, for that is the way you keep it alive.
I forget, it is washed away forever.
If you don't let go, it will haunt you and you will not be able to go forward.
I love you and I want you to go forward and enjoy your life to the fullest.
That is what I died for; it was not in vain.
So, My child learn from what you have gone through and let it make you a stronger person because of it
You are and overcomer in Me

1st John 1:9

If we confess our sins, He is faithful and just to forgive us (our) sins and to cleanse us from all unrighteousness.

365 Day Devotional...God still speaks today...John 10:27

DAILY ENCOURAGING WORDS...*TO LIVE BY*

October 17th

Arise and shine for the Glory Light of Jesus has come!
Have you not heard that My Word is your life's guideline?
Take My Word and put it before your eyes and read it so
that My Word will overtake you and change you into the
person that I have preordained you to be even before the
foundation of this world.

As you put time aside for My Word, you will see the
changes take place in you.

Do not be just hearers but ye be doers also of My Word.
Put it into practice and stand on My Word in all things for it
will never fail you.

Let it build up your faith.

As you partake of it daily, it will renew you and make you
strong to experience the joy, and peace that will flood your
spirit and renew your mind.

My Word is the food for your spirit to become strong just
as you eat food in the natural, to make your body strong.
As you eat daily, of My Word, you will become strong and
healthy, both in Spirit and in body.

Jerimiah 29:11

For I know the thoughts I think to towards you, says the
Lord, thoughts of peace and not of evil, to give you an
expected end.

DAILY ENCOURAGING WORDS...*TO LIVE BY*

October 18th

Arise and shine for the Glory Light of Jesus is come!
Praise Me, praise Me, and move into Me this day.
Let this day be full of expectations for what your God can do for you.
I AM working in every situation that you have put before Me this day.
You cannot see how I AM doing it in the Spirit, just know that I AM doing it.
I work in the Spirit first and then it is manifested in the natural realm.
Be in faith, believing all that I say I will do.
Rejoice and walk in My Peace, for you shall receive all that you have asked for.
Remember you serve a Mighty God that is not limited.
I AM not in a box.
I AM God Almighty, the Creator of the Heavens and the Earth and all that is in it.
I take the impossible and turn it into the possible.
So, when you ask, ask big, way beyond what you think, or you can do for yourself.
I long to bless you beyond your wildest dreams, trust Me.

1st John 5:14

And this is the confidence that we have in Him, that, if we ask anything according to His Will, He heareth us.

DAILY ENCOURAGING WORDS...*TO LIVE BY*

October 19th

Arise and shine for the Glory Light of Jesus has come!

Come My child and walk with Me in My Glory Light, for in My Light is freedom and peace, joy, and love.

All these things keep you fulfilled, and the darkness must flee from you.

It doesn't mean that you don't have to face problems, but it does mean that you can face your problems with power, and you have the strength to deal with these problems to overcome them.

You become stronger each time you allow Me to be continually in your life.

Take one day at a time.

You can walk in My Glory Light each day for I live within you.

The way to do this is to always let Me be in the forefront of your life.

Always surrendering to Me daily, for you cannot do it on your own.

Only walking in Me.

I AM always with you, no matter where you go.

You can always trust Me to carry you through.

Philippians 2:13

For it is God which worketh in you both to will and to do of His good pleasure.

365 Day Devotional...God still speaks today...John 10:27

DAILY ENCOURAGING WORDS...*TO LIVE BY*

October 20th

Arise and shine for the Glory Light of Jesus has come!
I have given you this day, walk in it knowing that the Love of the Father is flowing in you, a love that will never stop, it is unconditional.
You can know that My Love goes into every part of your life, for I care about you living your life whole and well, living your life out with all that I have for you.
You need not wonder how you are going to make ends meet, for I AM your God that shall meet all your needs according to My Glory by My Son (Christ Jesus).
Put your trust in Me and all will be well with you.
When you live a life close to and in Me, you will want for nothing, for this is My goal for you.
I want all My children to know that this is what I want for all. t
You belong to Me, and I watch over you continually.
Let your heart be filled with Me.
Praise Me and be thankful for all the things that I have blessed you with, big or small, there is no difference to Me.
I only ask that you believe.

Jeremiah 31:3

The Lord hath appeared of old unto Me. Yea, I have loved thee with an everlasting love; therefore, with lovingkindness have I crown thee.

365 Day Devotional...God still speaks today...John 10:27

DAILY ENCOURAGING WORDS...*TO LIVE BY*

October 21st

Arise and shine for the Glory Light of Jesus has come!
Am I not faithful to bring what My Word declares?
I have spoken My Word forth and watched over it, to see that what I have said would come to pass.
I AM that same God, I cannot change.
I AM the same yesterday and today and forever.
My Love for you does not change.
Everyday is the same when it comes to My children.
I look upon you and see My sons and daughters and My Love burns for all.
I AM no respecter of persons.
Reach out to Me and know that I always hear the prayers of My children and I do answer them.
It may not be the answer that you want at this time, but I know what is best for you.
Sometimes My children ask amiss, but they do not pray according to My Will, and I do not answer unless it lines up with My Word.
So, be careful to pray according to My Word and believe that you will have it and it will come to pass.

John 15:7

If ye abide in Me, and My Word abides in you, ye shall ask what ye will and it shall be done unto you.

DAILY ENCOURAGING WORDS...*TO LIVE BY*

October 22nd

Arise and shine for the Glory Light of Jesus has come!
Come into My presence and spend time with Me.
Let My presence saturate your whole being.
I AM, is all that you need.
Look to Me and surrender all.
It is not in your power to face and have all the answers that you need for all situations in your life.
But the power is in and through Me that can dismantle all situations that come your way.
It does not matter what they are.
Stay in My presence and ask of Me and trust Me, you will be able to live for Me, no matter the situation.
I AM your all sufficient One, there is no other.
Praise Me and walk in faith and know that you are always safe in My presence.
It is My presence for I live within you, through My Holy Spirit.
Now trust Me in all things.

Psalm 34:19
Many are the afflictions of the righteous, but the Lord delivers him out of them all.

DAILY ENCOURAGING WORDS...*TO LIVE BY*

October 23rd

Arise and shine for the Glory Light of Jesus has come!
Let the Joy of the Lord operate in your life this day.
The Joy of the Lord is your strength,
Be aware when the evil one (Satan), the enemy of your soul
will come to try to steal, kill and destroy you and keep you
from the Joy of the Lord working in your life.
Be aware of your thought life and every word you say.
There is power in the tongue, both life and death.
My child, you need to be continually watching what you
think or say, for it will determine the course of your life.
My desire for you is to look to Me and ask for help to guard
your tongue.
It is possible to do this through the Holy Spirit.
He will help you and teach you all truth.

Proverbs 18:21
Death and life are in the power of the tongue and they that
love it shall eat the fruit thereof.

DAILY ENCOURAGING WORDS...*TO LIVE BY*

October 24th

Arise and shine for the Glory Light of Jesus has come!
Put your hand into the Hand of the nail scarred Hands,
that is always open to you.
I will lead you and guide you through the rough times in your life.
When you put all your life in My hands, there is no worry or fear for I see where you are to go, and I lead you that way as you trust in Me to take you all the way to the end.
The end is to be with Me forever in Eternity.
Eye has not seen, nor ear heard what I have prepared for you.
Strive to be willing to surrender every part of your life to Me so that I can work in you to bring you to a place in Me.
I AM the only way that you can achieve the life I have destined for you.
Live one day at a time, and always keep your eyes on Me and learn My ways through the Written Word.
My Word will wash you clean.
Walk in My ways and you will be blessed

1st Corinthians 2:9

But as it is written, eye hath not seen, nor ear heard, neither have entered into the heart of man the things which God hath prepared for them that love Him.

365 Day Devotional...God still speaks today...John 10:27

DAILY ENCOURAGING WORDS...*TO LIVE BY*

October 25th

Arise and shine for the Glory Light of Jesus has come!
Step out of darkness into My Glorious Light.
Leave the things of this world behind and walk straight
ahead in the path that is lit up with My Light.
My Light leads to a full and prosperous life.
There is no room on this path for old way and thoughts.
I have brought you out of the worlds ways of doing things
and I AM changing you into a new person that will walk and
learn My ways of doing things.
These ways are not of the flesh but of the Spirit.
You will learn to trust Me and praise Me for what I have
done for you.
This life is a walk of faith and, a Love walk.
You will learn to walk in My Love, to share with others and
to show forth the goodness of the Father's Love.
The Father's Love is unconditional, so you should also love
people unconditional as I do.

1st John 2:15

Love not the world, neither the things that are in the world.
If any man love the world, the love of the Father is not in him.

DAILY ENCOURAGING WORDS...*TO LIVE BY*

October 26th

Arise and shine for the Glory Light of Jesus has come!
Come and walk in My Footsteps.
I have already gone before you and prepared the way for you.
Learn of Me and press into Me, take My hand and I will lead you all the way through.
Sometimes the way is rough and rocky but have no fear for I AM with you.
I will give you the strength and power to overcome.
Ask for My Wisdom, Knowledge and Understanding so that you will be able to choose what is right for you.
Be not quick to make decisions until you ask and use the tools that I have given you.
Let My Peace be your guide in all things.
When you do this, you are walking in My Footsteps.
Always be aware of what is going on around you, for I AM there to cheer you on.
I love you with an everlasting love.

John 14:27

Peace, I leave with you, My Peace I give unto you, not as the world giveth, give I unto you.
Let not your heart be troubled, neither let it be afraid.

365 Day Devotional...God still speaks today...John 10:27

October 27th

Arise and shine for the Glory Light of Jesus has come!
Come My child and watch and see My Hand move on your behalf today.
I see what need you have put before Me, I will provide, for My Word says that I AM is your Provider.
I care about every part of your life.
It is good that you believe in Me as your Provider.
Continue to look to Me and put Me first in everything you do.
When you do this, the way is also open to you and you will not fail in anything that you put your hand to, for I AM the One that guides you and gives you the knowledge to do it.
Do not lean on your own understanding for it will fail you.
Always put Me first and lean on Me, for I will not fail you.
Take Me at My Word and praise Me and trust Me in all parts of your life.
You are My child and I love you.

Micah 7:7
Therefore, I will look unto the Lord, I will wait for the God of my Salvation, my God will hear me.

October 28th

Arise and shine for the Glory Light of Jesus has come!
When you are weary, come apart from everyone and everything and let Me fill you up to overflowing.
My strength will put you back on track for the walk of life that I have planned for you.
When you let yourself get overtired because of the things you think need to be done in your day, you lose perspective of what really is going on in your life.
Remember to let My Spirit lead you and give you wisdom to do what needs to be done, first for Me, and then everything else will fall into place.
I want you to learn to lean on Me and trust Me for everything in your life.
Let Me be your only source and see what I will do in your life.
Remember I was the One who planned your life in the beginning, and I will see you through to the end.

Psalm 31:21
Be of good courage, and He shall strengthen your heart, all ye that hope in the Lord.

DAILY ENCOURAGING WORDS...*TO LIVE BY*

October 29th

Arise and shine for the Glory Light of Jesus has come!
Do not put your trust in man for your happiness.
Man is not capable of fulfilling your heart's desire, or able to bring you satisfaction.
So, look to the One that longs to do this for you.
I AM the only One that knows what you are feeling and wanting to be accepted for who you are.
Come to Me for all your wants to be fulfilled in a way that really counts.
I know everything about you, remember that I made you and truly I AM the only one who can bring you to fullness that I want for you.
What does it matter what others think about you.
If I am for you, who can be against you.
Press into Me and tell Me all that is going on with you.
I truly love you unconditionally.

Romans 8:31
What shall we then say to these things? If God be for us, who can be against us?

365 Day Devotional...God still speaks today...John 10:27

DAILY ENCOURAGING WORDS...*TO LIVE BY*

October 30th

Arise and shine for the Glory Light of Jesus has come!
Come and go with Me to My Father's House.
There is a preparation work to be done here on earth.
Everyday you work on getting ready for going to My Father's House.
Each day surrender all to Me, spirit, soul, and body.
As you do this; you allow the Holy Spirit to do the work in you that needs to be done.
The flesh must be laid down so that the Spirit will rise in you, this process is done over time.
You must always trust Me.
You do your part, and I will do the rest.
It is a daily thing, repeatedly until your time on this earth is over.
So, My child be willing everyday to lay down your life and take up Mine.
There is nothing that can stop you from finishing the goal, that has been set before you.
All is well My child.

John 14:3

And if I go and prepare a place for you, I will come again, and receive you unto Myself that where I AM (there) you may be also.

365 Day Devotional...God still speaks today...John 10:27

DAILY ENCOURAGING WORDS...*TO LIVE BY*

October 31st

Arise and shine for the Glory Light of Jesus has come!
Come and walk with Me.
Your pathway of life is already laid out before you.
Press into Me and allow Me to lead you and show you the way you should go.
My Light is a path unto your feet.
If you concentrate on My Glory Light, you will not fall into darkness, for there is no darkness in Me.
It is only when you fail to keep your eyes on Me, that you will stumble and fall to the wayside.
Commit yourself to follow Me daily, it is a walk of commitment.
You no longer own your own life, for you gave Me your life and permission to work out My ways in your life.
You cannot walk in the flesh and reap in the Spirit.
My goal for you is to always walk in the Spirit.
You are called to walk in My Spirit, which is totally living in My Kingdom.
When you decide to live in My Spirit, you will see the shift change in your life for the best, to come up higher in Me.
Choose a higher calling and be Blessed.

Galatians 6:8

For he that soweth to his flesh, reap corruption, but he that soweth to the Spirit shall of the Spirit reap life everlasting.

DAILY ENCOURAGING WORDS...*TO LIVE BY*

NOVEMBER

Psalm 107:1

O give thanks unto the LORD, for he is good: for his mercy endureth for ever.

365 Day Devotional...God still speaks today...John 10:27

DAILY ENCOURAGING WORDS...*TO LIVE BY*

November 1st

Arise and shine for the Glory Light of Jesus has come!
Out of the belly shall flow rivers of living waters.
That is where My Spirt, the Holy Spirit resides in you.
He is ever present, just waiting on you to ask for His help in time of need.
If you will give Him your time and attention, He will direct you in the way you should go and what you should do in every situation that you face.
He cannot help you if you do not consult Him in your everyday life.
He longs and waits for you to come into a relationship with Him, inviting Him to be part of your life.
He wants to become your friend.
Will you allow Him to do this?
He is the power you need to walk out your walk with Me.
You cannot do it by yourself, only with Him.

John 7:38
He that believeth on Me, as the scripture hath said, out of his belly shall flow rivers of living waters.

365 Day Devotional...God still speaks today...John 10:27

DAILY ENCOURAGING WORDS...*TO LIVE BY*

November 2nd

Arise and shine for the Glory Light of Jesus has come!
Let go and let My Holy Spirit take over every part of your life.
I want all of you not just some of you.
You cannot walk in the fullness that I have for you for you block it when you still hold back portions of your life.
Learn to give all and know that I will take care of you everyday of your life.
I do not leave when the going gets rough.
This is when you should look to Me more and more.
Your strength comes from Me.
You can not handle your life without My Holy Spirit that lives inside of you.
He never sleeps, He is always working on your behalf.
Continue to put My Word into your heart, so that you will be standing on what My Word says.
This is where the power is, My Word.
Speak forth My Word over your life and believe it.

2nd Samuel 22.31
As for God, this way is perfect; the Word of the Lord is tried. He is a buckler to all them that trust in Him.

November 3rd

Arise and shine for the Glory Light of Jesus has come.
Take My Hand and walk out this day with Me.
Lean on Me for I AM your Strength, your Joy, Peace, and Comforter.
I AM here for you; all you must do is ask and receive from Me.
I AM always with you, and I will never leave you.
When you live in Me, and I in you, there is no room for anything else.
So, let you of all things that would stop the flow from Me.
You cannot live two different lives and expect to have a life of peace and joy.
You either live in one or the other.
Choose life, for there is no other way to have what you truly want and be fully complete, it is all in Me.
So, I say, choose this day which way you will go.
Choose wisely.

Deuteronomy 30:19
I call Heaven and earth to record this day against you (that) I have set before you life and death, blessing and cursing, therefore choose life, that both thou and thy seed may live.

DAILY ENCOURAGING WORDS...*TO LIVE BY*

November 4th
Arise and shine for the Glory Light of Jesus has come!
Good morning My child.
I AM pleased that you are spending time with Me this morning.
It delights Me so.
You will need to do this on a regular base, for your adversary the devil (Satan) goes around as a roaring lion.
He is looking for weak ones that have not prepared for the day.
You need to ask the Holy Spirit to strengthen you for your day, for you know not what is ahead of you.
Praise and thanksgiving will open the door to Me.
Worship Me in Spirit and Truth.
Nothing moves Me more than the praises of My people.
There is power in your praises that comes from your heart.
It is pure and unadulterated praises.
Put aside that time with Me and I will move mightily on your behalf, and each time you do this, I will take you higher and higher in Me, from Glory to Glory.

1st Peter 5:8
Be sober, be vigilant, because your adversary the Devil, as a roaring lion, walketh about, seeking whom he may devour.

DAILY ENCOURAGING WORDS...*TO LIVE BY*

November 5th

Arise and shine for the Glory Light of Jesus has come!
Come, walk with Me.
We will walk together hand in hand.
You are My child.
Tell Me the concerns that are on your mind.
I AM interested in every area of your life.
Do not bottle up things inside of you which will only cause stress to take over which will cause the flow between us to stop.
Stress causes you to look at your problems and then worry starts to take place in your mind and opens the door for the fear and anxiety and pulls you out of faith.
When you are outside of faith, My Hands are tied, and I cannot do anything.
I work only in the realm of faith.
So, you must be careful to stay in faith and walk in love.
It is so important to keep your eyes on Me and know that I AM always here for you.

Deuteronomy 31:8
And the Lord, He (it is) that doth go before thee, He will be with thee, He will not fail thee, neither forsake thee; fear not, neither be dismayed.

DAILY ENCOURAGING WORDS...*TO LIVE BY*

November 6th

Arise and shine for the Glory Light of Jesus has come!
Go forth in the power and might of your God.
There is nothing that can't be done, faith believing in the name of Jesus.
Jesus is the Name above all other names, everything must bow to the Name of Jesus.
Through the resurrection of Jesus, you have the power within you to overcome all things.
I say to you this day to walk in Me and do many great things for My Kingdom.
You no longer live for yourself.
So, let My will be done in you., so you will be able to go forth and do mighty things for Me.
You need not fear, for Greater is He that is within you than he that is in the world.
It is time to go forth and show the world that you are full of My Power and Might.
I have called you to be great for Me in this dying world.
I AM with you and will guide you all the way.

1st John 1:1

Ye are of God, little children, and have overcome them: because greater is He that is in you, than he that is in the world.

365 Day Devotional...God still speaks today...John 10:27

DAILY ENCOURAGING WORDS...*TO LIVE BY*

November 7th

Arise and shine for the Glory Light of Jesus has come!
Walk in My Light, in My Light you will be able to see clearly and will be able to walk in the way that I have predestined just for you.
I have chosen you for a special calling that only you can do.
I have put within you all that is needed to complete your journey and your calling.
Everything has been put in place.
You need to seek My face and spend time in My Word for there you will find what you need to accomplish what needs to be done to fulfill what I have for you.
Take the time and spend it with Me, praising and showing Me honor and as you do this, it also builds you up spiritually.
This is a Spiritual lifestyle.
You must live it everyday.
You no longer depend on the flesh or walk in the flesh.
Keep your eyes on Me, I will see you through.

Philippians 4:13
I can do all things through Christ Which strengthens me.

DAILY ENCOURAGING WORDS...*TO LIVE BY*

November 8th

Arise and shine for the Glory Light of Jesus has come!
It is a good thing to put your life into My Hands.
So, trust Me and lean on Me for I have planned your footsteps from the beginning.
Therefore, your life will line up with what I have for you if you allow My Hand to guide you and show you the way.
First it is surrendering your whole life to Me, not holding back anything.
It is done in the Spirit realm first, and then walking it out in the natural.
Withhold nothing for what you hold back will trip you later.
I AM calling for all that concerns you, so that you can live a life of peace; joy and walk in My Love.
There is no other way.
It is your choice.
The flesh is weak, but My Spirit is strong.
Rely on My Spirit and He will always be there for you.
All you must do is ask Me, My child.

Proverbs 16:3
Commit thy works unto the Lord, and thy thoughts shall be established.

DAILY ENCOURAGING WORDS...*TO LIVE BY*

November 9th

Arise and shine for the Glory Light of Jesus has come!
Rest in Me, My child.
Take heart and know that all is well.
I watch over you and I know everything that takes place every moment of your day.
When things get you down and you are overwhelmed and cannot seem to put things together, that is the time to lift your voice to Me an put all things into My Hands.
I will show you the way out.
Do not ponder over your problems but come to Me from the beginning.
When you wait and your mind seems to run away on you, you lose sight of Me.
This is when Satan will try and get a foothold on you.
Do not let him do this, lift your head and begin to praise Me for there is power in your praise.
Always have a thankful heart and give honor to Me.

Psalm 27:14
Wait on the Lord; be of good courage, and He shall strengthen thine heart; wait, I say, on the Lord.

365 Day Devotional...God still speaks today...John 10:27

DAILY ENCOURAGING WORDS...*TO LIVE BY*

November 10th

Arise and shine for the Glory Light of Jesus has come!
Run your race with expectations of what I can do in your life.
Put Me at the helm and let Me direct your path.
I see what is ahead of you, so allow Me to go and make the crooked way straight.
There are many things that Satan throws at you to try and get your attention to get you off your path.
It is important to stay focused on Me, for I AM the Light of your path.
Be grounded in My Word, My Word is a Light unto your path.
Work on speaking My word forth into every situation in your life, no matter what the situation is.
My Word has answers to every situation.
This is why it is so important to know what My Word says to allow My Word to lead you.
My Word will only lead you to truth.

Psalm 119:130
The entrance of Thy Words giveth Light, it giveth understanding unto the simple.

November 11th

Arise and shine for the Glory Light of Jesus has come!
Let not your heart be troubled, for I AM with you.
Put aside all things that do not line up with My Word, for I AM pure and there is no darkness in Me.
That is what My children need to strive for.
My Word declares that you are to be Holy as I AM holy.
You are well able to obtain this goal, for you have the Holy Spirit within you, who gives you the power to work toward this.
He will help you to strip away all things that are not lining up with My Word.
You cannot reach this goal by yourself.
This is why I sent My Holy Spirit to mankind.
It is a choice you must make and stick with this choice until you and the Holy Spirit has accomplished what is needed.
He is always with you.

Titus 2:12
Teaching us that, denying ungodliness, and worldly lusts, we should live soberly, righteously and Godly, in this present world.

DAILY ENCOURAGING WORDS...*TO LIVE BY*

November 12th

Arise and shine for the Glory Light of Jesus has come!

Press into Me this day!

Open to Me, so I can pour into you all I have for you today.

I want to renew your strength and give you My Peace that surpasses the world's peace.

The world's peace comes and goes with the changes of each situation.

It is up and down, but the Peace I give unto you is stable.

It never waivers unless you step out of it.

Learn to trust in Me and know that I do not waiver.

I have given you My Holy Spirit to lead and guide you in all things in every part of your life.

Give Him permission to work in you and allow Him to teach you and give you His Wisdom to conquer anything that arises in your life.

Take joy in knowing that you can always lean on the Holy Spirit for help no matter what it is or where you are.

Step out in faith and know that all is well.

John 14:26

But the Comforter, the Holy Spirit, whom the Father will send in My Name, He shall teach you all things, and bring all things to your remembrance, whatsoever I have said unto you.

DAILY ENCOURAGING WORDS...*TO LIVE BY*

November 13th

Arise and shine for the Glory Light of Jesus has come!
Step out in faith and believe that what you are praying has already started to manifest.
I have heard your prayers, and I will do what you have asked for.
Keep praising Me and trusting Me no matter what it looks like.
Satan would like to get you out of faith and walking in fear.
He tries to get you to think about the problem and get your eyes off Me.
If you let him do this, you will stop the flow of what I have already started.
So, put a guard about your mind so that Satan cannot hinder what I AM doing.
He is out to steal your faith for without faith you will not be able to move forward in your walk with Me.

James 1:6

But let him ask in faith, nothing wavering. For he that wavereth is like a wave of the sea driven with the wind and tossed.

DAILY ENCOURAGING WORDS...*TO LIVE BY*

November 14th

Arise and shine for the Glory Light of Jesus has come!
Lay down your old life and step into your new life with Me.
Your old life was full of darkness but your new life in Me is full of Light.
Now you will be able to see the path that I have created just for you.
Keep your eyes on Me so that you can see what I want for you.
Trust Me in everything that pertains to your life.
I want you to succeed to the fullest capacity of your life.
I have so much for you.
You must believe and receive this so that you will achieve the fullness as to what I have for you in your life.
You do not walk out your life alone.
I have sent My Holy Spirit to help you and guide you all the way through.
He is always with you and will never leave you.

2nd Corinthians 5:17

Therefore, if any man be in Christ, he is a new creature, old things are passed away, behold all things are become new.

DAILY ENCOURAGING WORDS...*TO LIVE BY*

November 15th

Arise and shine for the Glory Light of Jesus has come!
Yes, I say, expect, expect, good things to happen this day.
Keep your eyes on Me and you will not miss them.
With an open heart, praise Me and be in thanksgiving, giving Me all honor and praise that is due to Me.
I do not share My Glory with no one.
I AM jealous of you and watch over you every moment of the day.
You are never out of My sight.
I AM working in you to bring you into the place that I want you to be so, continue to surrender all to Me.
All I ask is that when you surrender all to Me, watch Me do the work in you that I have destined for you.
It is Spiritual work first and then begins to change the way you do things.
You will truly see the work being done in you.
This is My will for you.
Just be willing to cooperate with Me.
Just remember, I will never leave you.

Psalm 37:4
Delight yourself in the Lord, and He will give you the desires of your heart.

DAILY ENCOURAGING WORDS...*TO LIVE BY*

November 16th

Arise and shine for the Glory Light of Jesus has come!
Have you not heard that I have said in My written Word, that I look over you and that I would take care of you?
There is nothing that I cannot do.
I see where you are at this very moment and what situation you are in.
I know that you think that it will not get much better, but I say that My Hand is working in the situation right now.
Train yourself to always look to Me and not think of your situation.
This only leads you to believe that it is hopeless, but it is not.
It is in My Hands, and you will see a great change in your situation.
Faith conquers all if you only believe in Me.
You are not able to change things around so allow Me to do it.
Do not tie My Hands by stepping out of faith.
Just believe and know that all is well.

Psalm 32:8
I will instruct thee and teach thee in the way which thou shalt go, I will guide thee with Mine eye.

DAILY ENCOURAGING WORDS...*TO LIVE BY*

November 17th

Arise and shine for the Glory Light of Jesus has come!
Let go and stand strong on My Word.
My Word is the strength for your life.
From My Word you will find an answer to everything that is upsetting your life.
There will always be troubles and situations arise in your life always take My Word and find the answer to deal with them.
You do not have the answer in your own strength nor does the world ways have the answers.
Go to My Word even when you do not have a problem.
The Word builds you up so that when situations come at you, you will be ready to handle these situations.
My Word is the food for your spirit.
My Holy Spirit lives within you.
He is full of wisdom and power to help you conquer the trials in your life.
The Word and the Holy Spirit work together to help you conquer life's trials.
The Holy Spirit will never fail you.

Luke 11:28
But He said, yea rather; blessed are they that hear the word of God and keep it.

365 Day Devotional...God still speaks today...John 10:27

DAILY ENCOURAGING WORDS...*TO LIVE BY*

November 18th

Arise and shine for the Glory Light of Jesus has come!
Seek My thoughts in all that you do.
Do not go ahead of Me nor linger behind Me.
When you are walking in the Spirit, it is very important to seek My Face and My Will for all and everything that pertains to your life.
When you are in the Spirit, the Holy Spirit will lead you and guide you in every step you need to take.
So, do not be anxious for anything, but enquire of the Holy Spirit.
When you are in doubt, that is the time to stop and take a good look at the situation and go to the Holy Spirit to see what He wants you to do.
He will never lead you astray.
It is very important to learn to trust Him in all things.
In the end, all things will come together, and you will be in peace.
This is the knowing that all is well.
There is no other way but to trust and obey.

Galatians 5:16
This I say then, walk in the Spirit and ye shall not fulfill the lust of the flesh.

DAILY ENCOURAGING WORDS...*TO LIVE BY*

November 19th

Arise and shine for the Glory Light of Jesus has come!
Let not your heart be troubled, only believe.
Look unto Me for I AM with you.
Tap into My Peace, for My Peace is within you.
When you walk in My Peace, there is no room for anything else.
When you are in My Peace, joy bubbles up from the depth of your soul.
That is when you can walk in Love and your faith begins to rise for you to see clearly again.
The way to hold onto your peace is to put My Word into your spirit, for it is food for your spirit.
Then your spirit releases what is needed to overcome what was troubling you in the first place.
Always feed on My Word, day in and day out.
Without My Word you will become weak and fall away from Me.
My Word strengthens you, so feed on it always.

John 14:27
Peace, I leave with you, My Peace I give unto you. I do not give you as the world gives. Do not let your heart be troubled and do not be afraid.

365 Day Devotional...God still speaks today...John 10:27

DAILY ENCOURAGING WORDS...*TO LIVE BY*

November 20th

Arise and shine for the Glory Light of Jesus has come!
Let praise, honor and Glory flow from your heart, this day.
Look to Me for all blessings flow from Me.
It is My desire to pour into your life this day.
That is My nature, in a loving and giving way.
I long to see My children walk in My Nature, out of a Loving Heart and out of a Loving Spirit, that My children would be so full of My Nature.
You would be living so close to Me, that your faith would rise, and you would be able to believe for anything that you wanted.
You would be fulfilling My desire for you.
To do this, there is a letting go of the old ways and turning everything of your life to Me.
That you would die to yourself and receive My ways for your life, in doing so I would be living in every part of your life.
We would become one as I have intended us to be.

John 17.23

I in them, and thou in Me, that they may be made perfect in Me, and that the world may know that Thou has sent Me, and hast loved them, as thou hast loved Me.

DAILY ENCOURAGING WORDS...*TO LIVE BY*

November 21st

Arise and shine for the Glory Light of Jesus has come!
Come into My presence and spend time with Me.
Let My presence saturate your whole being.
I AM is all that you need.
Look to Me and give Me all.
It is not in your power to do and have the answer that you need for all situations in your life, but the power in and through Me that is able to dismantle these situations.
It does not matter what they are.
Stay in My presence and ask of Me and trust Me, you will be able to live for Me no matter what.
I AM your all sufficient ONE, there is no other.
Praise Me and walk in faith and know that you are always safe in My presence.
It is possible to be in My presence for I live within you, through My Holy Spirit.

Psalm 34:19
Many are the afflictions of the righteous, but the Lord delivers him out of them all.

November 22nd

Arise and shine for the Glory Light of Jesus has come!
Did I not say that I would do the work in you, to cleanse you from all unrighteousness?
This needs to be done so that I can take you higher in Me.
Each time you give something over to Me that is weighing you down spiritually, I can do the work and you grow more in My ways.
Do not stop until you have surrendered all your past to Me.
Once the past is taken care of, you will be able to leave the past behind and walk into your new destiny that I have ordained for you.
The past will hold you captive if you let it.
This is why you must give it all to Me and I will set you free.
Little by little it will be done.
You cannot handle having it done all at once, this is why it is done over time.
Just continue to surrender to Me and trust Me in all things.

2nd Corinthians 3:18

But we all, with open face beholding as a glass, the Glory of the Lord, are changed into the same images from Glory to Glory, even as by the Spirit of the Lord.

DAILY ENCOURAGING WORDS...*TO LIVE BY*

November 23rd

Arise and shine for the Glory Light of Jesus has come!
Take Mt Hand, for it is always stretched out to you.
If your hand is in Mine, there is no need to fear anything.
There is no fear in Me.
I AM love and it will flow down to you from Me.
The connection will always be there.
Things of this world cannot touch you when you are grounded in Me.
Know who you are in Me, and that the Father's love is forever, for He is love.
Let this love saturate your whole being and know that all is well.
No matter what you face, My love will pull you through.
Everyday that you live, know that you are loved and protected by that love.
It will never leave you.
Love is the strongest thing in this world, it will overcome everything. Walk in it.

1st John 4:16

And we have known and believed the Love that God hath to us. God is Love, and He that dwelleth in love dwelleth in God, and God in him.

DAILY ENCOURAGING WORDS...*TO LIVE BY*

November 24th
Arise and shine for the Glory Light of Jesus has come!
Here it is another day.
Let this day be filled with goodness of your God.
Look to Me and call upon Me for everything that you need for this day.
I AM is in this day for you, just waiting on you to call out to Me.
I have all the answers to what you need.
Tell Me what you want.
Release your faith and believe and receive that which you are wanting.
Thank Me and praise Me, Glorify Me.
You live one day at a time.
Do not live in the past and do not visit the future.
I AM a now God.
Live in the now.
Center in on Me and give Me all that you have.
I love you unconditionally.

1st John 5:15
And if we know that He hears us, whatsoever we ask, we know that we have the petition that we desired of Him.

November 25th

Arise and shine for the Glory Light of Jesus has come!
You are My Child; you are highly esteemed in My eyes.
You were bought with My Blood.
You are very important to Me.
I see you as a rough diamond.
I will cause you to be changed into My image.
You will be changed from Glory to Glory.
The more you let go of your desires and your will and let Me put the desires that I want to put in you, to accomplish My Will and desire for you.
You will be able to walk with your head held high and no matter what troubles come your way, you will shine as a perfect diamond and all will see that you truly are a different person, than you were before you allowed Me to transform you into the person you were ordained to be.
My love for you is everlasting to everlasting.

2nd Corinthians 3:18

But we all, with open face beholding as in a glass the Glory of the Lord, are changed into the same image from Glory to Glory even as by the Spirit of the Lord.

DAILY ENCOURAGING WORDS...*TO LIVE BY*

November 26th

Arise and shine for the Glory Light of Jesus has come!
Sit and be still in your thoughts.
The mind is a powerful thing, that is where all things are decided.
It is very important to be mindful to what is going on in your mind.
The mind can contain a lot of different thoughts at one time.
It is important to decipher what is going on in your mind.
This is where you need the Holy Spirit that lives within you to help you to discern what is good or bad.
The enemy of your soul works in your mind to deceive you and pull you off track.
Destroy the works of the enemy before the thoughts are deeply rooted in your mind.
Satan comes to steal, kill, and destroy the good things that I am doing in your life.
Be diligent and cast down all bad thoughts and clear your mind of them.

2nd Corinthians 10:5

Casting down imaginations, and every high thing that exalteth itself against the knowledge of God and bringing into captivity every thought to the obedience of Christ.

November 27th

Arise and shine for the Glory Light of Jesus has come!
Rest in Me, My child.
Take heart and know that all is well.
I watch over you and I know everything that takes place every moment of your day.
When things get you down and you are overwhelmed and cannot seem to pull things together, that is the time to lift your voice to Me and put all into My hands.
I will show you the way out.
Do not ponder over your problems but come to Me at the beginning.
When you wait and your mind seems to run away on you and you lose your sight of Me, that is when Satan will try and get a foothold on you.
Do not let him do this.
Lift your head and begin to Praise Me for there is power in your praises.
Always have a thankful heart and give honor to Me.

Psalm 27:14
Wait on the Lord, be of good courage, and He shall strengthen thine heart, wait, I say on the Lord.

November 28th

Arise and shine for the Glory Light of Jesus has come!
It is so important to trust Me in all things.
When you speak forth words that are not of faith, then you are leaning towards your flesh and your own understanding.
For what comes out of your mouth is what determines whether you are in faith or in the flesh.
They cannot work together.
They are the opposite of one another.
Faith is what works in the Kingdom of God, without it you cannot tap into benefits of the Kingdom of God.
Watch what you think upon and what you are saying.
Take watch over your mind, so that you will not speak forth words that will hinder your walk with Me.

Romans 8:6
For to be carnally minded (is) death, but to be spiritually minded (is) life and peace

DAILY ENCOURAGING WORDS...*TO LIVE BY*

November 29th

Arise and shine for the Glory Light of Jesus has come!
My child learn to leave all concerns at the foot of the cross.
Every part of your life is in My Hands, and I will never let you go, or see you without.
Do not let the enemy of your soul tell you lies and get you to the point where you are thinking that you are not loved by Me, for that is truly a lie from the enemy.
Do you think that all that I went through was in vain.
Every drop of blood that flowed from My Body was for you.
If it was only, you in this vast world, I would have done it just for you.
My love is flowing out to the whole world.
I love mankind, for they are My creation.
I would desire that non should perish.
I have made the way clear so that all mankind could come to the Cross and repent and walk in My love daily.
Never give up, keep on looking to Me, for I AM the One that will lead you and keep you.

Romans 5:8
But God commandeth His love towards us, in that while we ever yet sinners, Christ died for us.

365 Day Devotional...God still speaks today...John 10:27

DAILY ENCOURAGING WORDS...*TO LIVE BY*

November 30th

Arise and shine for the Glory Light of Jesus has come!
Let Me lead you and show you the way that you should go.
There is so much happening all around you and if you are not careful, you would be carried away by what is happening around you.
You need to be totally filled up with My Word and letting My Word show you what direction you should walk in,
It is the only true guideline to follow.
Let My Holy Spirit teach you, for He is your helper and guide.
Lean on Him for everything that you need.
He has your answer to what is happening to you in every part of your life.
Trust that small still voice, that speaks to you from within.

1st John 4:13
Hereby know we that we dwell in Him, and He in us, because He hath given us of His Spirit.

DAILY ENCOURAGING WORDS...*TO LIVE BY*

DECEMBER

Luke 2:14

Glory to God in the highest, and on earth peace, good will toward men.

365 Day Devotional...God still speaks today...John 10:27

DAILY ENCOURAGING WORDS...*TO LIVE BY*

December 1st

Arise and shine for the Glory Light of Jesus has come!
Walk in the stillness of your spirit man.
Your spirit is intertwined with My Holy Spirit.
Train your ear to hear what your spirit is saying to you.
Tune out all other things in your life and concentrated on what is going on in the inside of you.
What goes on inside is the life that is between you, and I
AM
That is more important than your outer life.
When you are in tune with Me, then you can connect with your outer life.
When the inner life is living the way, you should with Me, then the outer life will line up with this, and you will treat others with love and respect.
You must treat others the way that you want to be treated.
This is walking in the Spirit.

1st Peter 3:4

But (let it be) the hidden man of the heart, in that which is not corruptible, (even the ornament) of a meek and quiet spirit, which is in the sight of God of great price.

DAILY ENCOURAGING WORDS...*TO LIVE BY*

December 2nd

Arise and shine for the Glory Light of Jesus has come!
Be still in your thoughts and know that I AM God.
Allow Me to work in you and through you, so that I can bring forth what I have put in you.
Yes, there is great potential in all My children.
The way for this to come forth is for My children to learn to surrender their lives to Me, daily and give Me permission to work their potential out in them.
It is done little by little, so do not get discouraged.
Be patient and know no matter what it looks like, just know that My Holy Spirit is doing the work in you.
You can't do the work, only My Holy Spirit knows what needs to be done and when it needs to be done.
So, rejoice and cooperate with Him.
You will see the results and so will others see it too.
This is done for the Glory of God.
For you are all called to do a special work in My Kingdom.

2nd Corinthians 3:18

But we all, with open face be holding as in a glass the Glory of God the Lord, are changed into the same image from Glory to Glory, even as by the Spirit of the Lord.

365 Day Devotional...God still speaks today...John 10:27

DAILY ENCOURAGING WORDS...*TO LIVE BY*

December 3rd

Arise and shine for the Glory Light of Jesus has come!
Leap for joy, in knowing that Salvation has come to you in its fullness.
All that you need or want is written within you.
Call it forth.
I have put it in you and My Holy Spirit is just waiting for you to come forth and ask for what you want.
Only you can cause it to happen.
Speak it forth and believe what My word says and receive it by faith.
When My Father spoke forth the Words to create, it was done.
So shall it be now, for I have not changed.
Speak the Word out of your mouth and release it by faith and believe and receive it and it shall be yours.
It is already done in the Spirit, that was My part, so now you do your part, and it shall be done.

2nd Corinthians 1.13
We having the same Spirit of faith, according as it is written I believed and therefore have I spoken, we also believe and therefore speak.

365 Day Devotional...God still speaks today...John 10:27

DAILY ENCOURAGING WORDS...*TO LIVE BY*

December 4th

Arise and shine for the Glory Light of Jesus has come!
Stand still and see the Hand of God work in your life this day.
Put aside all the things that would cause the flow of My Power from flowing through you.
It is important to center your mind on Me and not other things to stop the flow.
You have the power to settle your mind.
Use this power within you which is the Holy Spirit.
Take time to connect with Him.
Without the power working in your, you become stagnant and cannot overcome anything that would come against you.
So, open to My Spirit and work with Him and together Mighty things will be accomplished in your life.
Trust Him.

Ephesians 4:30
And grieve not the Holy Spirit of God, whereby ye are sealed unto the day of redemption.

DAILY ENCOURAGING WORDS...*TO LIVE BY*

December 5th

Arise and shine for the Glory Light of Jesus has come!
Walk with Me this day.
Let Me lead you and show you the way that you should go.
Everything that you need is already planted within your spirit.
I put it there long before you were put in your mother's womb.
So, you are already equipped to walk out your journey with Me.
It is a process, and day by day as you allow Me to work in you by My Holy Spirit, He will teach you how and what to do.
You must take My written Word and read it and study it so you will be able to stand upon it and receive all that you need for your life, to live in faith and act upon My Word.
Take it and apply it to your life and walk out your walk in the fullness that I have for you.

Luke 11:28
But He said, yea rather, blessed are they that hear the Word of God, and keep it.

DAILY ENCOURAGING WORDS...*TO LIVE BY*

December 6th

Arise and shine for the Glory Light of Jesus has come!
Come to Me when you are weary, and I will give you rest.
There is a place in Me that you can rest and be totally safe.
This is in the secret place.
There is total peace there.
The secret place is in My presence.
When you totally abandoned everything and spend time in worshipping Me, you will be filled with My Peace, and you will be transformed in My presence.
Each day put aside a time for you and Me and together we will become as one.
This is how you grow in stature in Me.
You become one with Me and your light will shine brighter and brighter for you are allowing Me to do the work in you and change you into the person you need to become that has already been destined for you.

Psalm 91:1
He that dwelleth in the secret place of the Most High shall abide under the shadow of the Almighty.

DAILY ENCOURAGING WORDS...*TO LIVE BY*

December 7th

Arise and shine for the Glory Light of Jesus has come.
Wait upon the Lord and He will renew your strength.
The joy of the Lord will carry you through your day.
When you are down and need to be refreshed, this is the time to trust in Me and allow Me to fill you up to overflowing.
Put aside the weight of the things of this world and turn to Me.
There is no other way.
It is only My Holy Spirit that lives within you, that can fill you up and lead you to the place in Me where you need to be.
You do not do things on your own but trust the Holy Spirit to work with you to become the person of faith.
Allow your faith to soar in Me and come up higher in Me.

Isaiah 40:31
They that wait upon the Lord, shall renew their strength, they shall mount up with wings of Eagles; they shall run and not be weary, walk and not faint.

365 Day Devotional...God still speaks today...John 10:27

DAILY ENCOURAGING WORDS...*TO LIVE BY*

December 8th

Arise and shine for the Glory Light of Jesus has come!
When you need answers for situations that arise everyday of your life, ask of Me and in faith believing that I have the answers for those situations to be taken care of.
You are not limited to what you can do in the natural, but I AM all powerful and all knowing.
I will give you all answers, and give you My Peace and Joy, while you are going through these problems.
Praise Me and trust Me always to help you, for I AM a prayer away.
My ears are always open to My children when they call upon My Name.
Be quick to come to Me, do not allow the enemy to work his way in and cause you to come into fear.
Fear is the opposite of faith.
I will always be with you and in you.
Stand on faith and always come to Me first.
Go about your day and be blessed.

1st John 5:15

And if we know that He hears us, whatsoever we ask, we know that we have the petitions that we desired of Him.

365 Day Devotional...God still speaks today...John 10:27

DAILY ENCOURAGING WORDS...*TO LIVE BY*

December 9th

Arise and shine for the Glory Light of Jesus has come!
Sit at My feet and learn of Me.
Each time you do this, you will begin to grow in your walk with Me, and as you grow, the interest that you have in the things of this world, you begin to lose your interest in them.
Things will just drop off.
You will become full of peace, and joy will bubble up within you, and you begin to see that you do not need the things that you thought you could not let go of in the past.
I AM the Light of the world.
You began to see the Light and it showed you the need to let go of the darkness that was holding you back.
Continue to learn of Me, through My Written Word and I will reveal its truth to you, and you will become a doer of My Word, not just to read but to do what is required.
My Word is the changing power for your life.

Psalm 119:11
Thy Word have I hid in my heart, that I might not sin against thee.

December 10th

Arise and shine for the Glory Light of Jesus has come!
Look up, lift your head up high and sing praises unto Me.
The Joy of the Lord is your strength.
As you sing unto Me, you are releasing power in your life to set you free.
It allows the Holy Spirit to work in you to set you free from all the things that are in your soul that hold you back from serving Me the way that I desire you to.
Singing unto Me makes you feel light and happy and clears the way for peace and joy to fill your whole being.
It pushes out darkness and any cloud of depression hanging over you, are driven from you.
Rejoice, rejoice, use the power of praise, and walk in My Joy and Peace, My children.

Psalm 9:2
I will be glad and rejoice in Thee; I will sing praises to Thy name, O Thou Most High.

December 11th

Arise and shine for the Glory Light of Jesus has come!
Have I not said that I would never leave you nor forsake you?
When you are troubled and cannot seem to see your way through your troubles, do not spend time trying to figure out which way to turn.
Come to Me right away and tell Me all that concerns you.
In doing so, it stops the door from being opened to allow Satan in to lead you the wrong way.
He is not for you but is against you.
He will try everything and anything to pull you away from Me.
You must be always on guard.
You will always be afflicted by the things coming against you, but you can overcome, for My Holy Spirit lives within you and He has all the answers.
Trust in Him and all will be well with you.

Psalm 9:10
And they that know thy name will put their trust in Thee; for thou Lord, has not forsaken them that seek Thee.

DAILY ENCOURAGING WORDS...*TO LIVE BY*

December 12th

Arise and shine for the Glory Light of Jesus has come!
Come to Me, you who are heavy laden, and I will give you rest.
Take My Yoke upon you for it is not burdensome.
I long to see you free from all burdens.
Bring them to Me and see what I will do for you.
It is in faith that you will do this.
When you say, I will surrender all to you and release it unto Me, then you will feel all the burdens roll off you and rest will come upon you.
You will walk in victory and your life will show the difference, the darkness has gone, and My Light will shine through you.
It is another level that you have come up to.
You are changed from Glory to Glory.
You need to be ever moving and never standing still.
I will see you through it all just put your trust in Me for there is no other than I.
I can do what needs to be done in your life and much more.

Matthew 11:29

Take My yoke upon you and learn of Me; for I AM meek and lowly in heart; and ye shall find rest unto your souls.

365 Day Devotional...God still speaks today...John 10:27

December 13th

Arise and shine for the Glory Light of Jesus has come!
Step down from trying to run your own life without letting My Holy Spirit help you.
In yourself you have no power to do what I have called you for.
This is why the Holy Spirit was given to you.
He is your Helper and Guide.
He sees all and knows all, so lean not on your own understanding, just surrender all to Him.
He is just waiting for you to ask for His help.
When you let Him guide you, there is no guessing.
He has all the answers.
He will never leave you nor forsake you.
Make the decision to lean on Him and call on Him every time you have a situation that you see no way out.
Learn to trust Him and you will see how well your life will be, when you surrender your life to Him.

1st Corinthians 6:19
What, know ye not that your body is the temple of the Holy Spirit (Ghost)
Which is in you, which ye have of God, and ye are not your own?

DAILY ENCOURAGING WORDS...*TO LIVE BY*

December 14th

Arise and shine for the Glory Light of Jesus has come!
I have come so that you might have life and have life more abundantly.
My desire for you is to walk in My fullness that I have for you.
I have laid out your life from the very beginning.
Your life is written down in My Book of Remembrance.
I know what you will do and say, what you will do every day.
You are My child and I have already provided for you.
Now you need to do your part and work with Me to bring all that I have for you, to bring it to pass in your life.
Walk in My righteousness and walk in faith and in My Love.
It is possible to walk in My Love through the Holy Spirit that lives within you.
He is the Power that will teach you how to line up your life with what My Word says.
My Spirit and My Word work hand in hand together.
Allow Him to take the reins of your life and trust Him to do the work with you.

Malachi 3:16

Then they that feared the Lord spake often one to another, the Lord hearkened, and heard it, and a Book of Remembrance was written before Him for them that feared the Lord, and thought upon His name.

DAILY ENCOURAGING WORDS...*TO LIVE BY*

December 15th

Arise and shine for the Glory Light of Jesus has come!
You see how important it is to walk in My Spirit.
Everything you need to walk the good fight of Faith is in Him.
Every time you need an answer to a situation, go to Him and inquire for the answer.
He will show you what needs to be done in your situation.
Create a relationship with Him, where you will be able to go to Him at any given time.
He is always waiting on you.
Talk to Him like you are talking to a friend.
He will answer you; He is always open to you.
Learn to go to Him in everything that you do.
You need to be aware of things that are happening all around you, harmful to you.
You will be able to trust the Holy Spirit to show you how to handle each situation.
This relationship can only be based on trust.
Trust Him.

Romans 8:14
For as many as are led by the Spirit of God, they are the sons of God.

December 16th

Arise and shine for the Glory Light of Jesus has come!
Do not put your trust in anyone or the things of this world.
When you do this, you are not trusting in Me for the very things that count in your life.
It doesn't matter what other people think.
It only matters what I think about you, and I AM the One that loves you unconditionally.
Come to Me for all that would be needed in your life, this very moment.
When you are sad, only turn to Me, for there is joy and peace for every part of your life, you can only find it in Me.
Not other people, for they themselves are not even satisfied within their own selves.
So, only look to Me and you will not be disappointed.

Colossians 3:2
Set your affections on things above, not on things on the earth.

DAILY ENCOURAGING WORDS...*TO LIVE BY*

December 17th

Arise and shine for the Glory Light of Jesus has come!
As you walk out your life daily and your eyes are centered upon Me, you see the goodness that flows out of Me.
I AM there every moment of your day; from the very moment you get up to the very moment you go to bed.
I AM continually watching over you, even when you are sleeping.
I never sleep, I AM always working in your life.
When you continually keep your eyes on Me, it keeps the enemy of your soul at bay, for you do not give him an open door to work in your life.
He cannot stand the Glory Light; therefore, he will not stay around you.
So, it is very important that you train your mind to think on the things of the Kingdom and My ways.
It is in the written Word.
It is your guideline for your life.
My Holy Spirit is always in you to teach you all things.
Only ask Him and depend on Him every moment.

1st Corinthians 2:16
For who hath known the mind of the Lord, that He may instruct him? But we have the mind of Christ.

DAILY ENCOURAGING WORDS...*TO LIVE BY*

December 18th

Arise and shine for the Glory Light of Jesus has come!
Follow Me and put Me first in your life and see the pieces of your life, to start to come together.

Your life is like a puzzle.

You do not start out with the whole picture.

You were broken, but when you gave your life to Me, you trusted Me to take your life and put the broken pieces back together so that your life would be formed for the purpose that I had already planned for you long ago before you were even born.

So, now day by day I AM still working in your life.

It is a walk of faith, and one day at a time.

Learning to put your life in My Hands each and everyday unto the day I take you home.

If you trust in My Love for you, you will be fulfilled and whole in every part of your life.

2nd Corinthians 5:17

Therefore, if any man (be) in Christ, (he is) a new creature; old things are passed away, behold, all things are become new.

DAILY ENCOURAGING WORDS...*TO LIVE BY*

December 19th

Arise and shine for the Glory Light of Jesus has come!
Let My Glory Light shine through you.
You are a vessel of Light for Me.
Your life no longer belongs to you.
You are bought with My Blood that I shed on the Cross at Calvary.
So, therefore My presence resides in you.
My presence is the Holy Spirit that lives with you.
He is the power in which you need to live your life in the manner that will honor Me.
So, righteousness will flow from your life.
You no longer live for yourself, but your life will show forth the attributes of Me.
Walk in My Love and show forth My Peace and be filled with My Joy.
These are the things that people will see and know that you are different than they.
This will show, and is what sets you apart from all others that do not know Me but need Me.

1st John 5:3
For this is the love of God, that we keep His commandments and His commandments are not grievous.

DAILY ENCOURAGING WORDS...*TO LIVE BY*

December 20th

Arise and shine for the Glory Light of Jesus has come!
Walk in My ways and you will be blessed.
My way is not hard for I have already gone before you and put all that you need into its place and provided all for you.
All you need to do is rely on My Strength and Power that is within you.
The Holy Spirit is that power.
He will always show you the way.
My written Word is your road map.
Take My Word and put it deep into your Spirit and speak it forth and believe it to do what it has said.
The power is in My written Word, you need to activate it by speaking it forward.
It is done by faith.
Watch and see what I will do for you.

Hebrews 4:12
For the Word of God is quick and powerful, and sharper than any tow edged sword, piercing even to the dividing asunder of soul and spirit, and of the joints and marrow, and is a discerner of the thoughts and intents of the heart.

365 Day Devotional...God still speaks today...John 10:27

DAILY ENCOURAGING WORDS...*TO LIVE BY*

December 21st

Arise and shine for the Glory Light of Jesus has come!
Walk in My ways, for that is the only way that will keep you going forward in the path of life, that has been laid out for you.
You did not plan your life; I did from the beginning.
I put desires in your heart, and they will be worked out with the help of My Holy Spirit that lives within.
He will teach you and lead you in the way you are to go.
If you will walk with the Holy Spirit and listen to Him, you will not fail, and your life will be worth while living.
My plan for your life is to succeed in every part of your life.
You will live a full and happy life.
You need to choose to surrender to the Holy Spirit and day by day walk with Him and you will see the difference that it makes in your life.

Proverbs 23:26
My son, give Me thine heart, and let thine eyes observe My ways.

365 Day Devotional...God still speaks today...John 10:27

DAILY ENCOURAGING WORDS...*TO LIVE BY*

December 22nd

Arise ad shine for the Glory Light of Jesus has come!
Let your day be filled with the power and strength that comes from Me.
Sing praise to Me and feel the joy rise within you.
Walk in My presence and let the Peace of God rule your day.
As you walk in My Peace, nothing can overtake you.
Always keep your eyes on Me.
I AM the rock that you stand upon.
I AM, the strength that you draw from.
I AM, is always with you.
Walk in this day knowing you are blessed and loved.

Colossians 3:15
And let the peace of God rule in your heart, to which also ye are called in one body, and be ye thankful.

DAILY ENCOURAGING WORDS...*TO LIVE BY*

December 23rd

Arise and shine for the Glory Light of Jesus has come!
I will lead you and be with you in all that you do.
As you learn to walk with Me and put your trust in Me, you will see the hand of the Lord move more and more in your life.
When you surrender your life for Mine, all things of the world will begin to drop from you, and you will begin to see the difference in yourself, and the Glory Light will shine in and through you and out to those around you.
This is My desire for you, to live a life of peace, joy, and righteousness.
So, I say lay down your life and take on Mine.
I will always be there for you.

Psalm 9:10
And they that know thy name will put their trust in Thee;
For Thou Lord, has not forsaken them that seek Thee.

DAILY ENCOURAGING WORDS...*TO LIVE BY*

December 24th

Arise and shine for the Glory Light of Jesus has come!
This is a blessed time of the year.
It gives Me great joy that My children come together all over the world to be in one accord, to honor Me and to put aside things that does not really matter to put others before themselves.
It is a time of year that joy wells up within My children.
A time of year to let My Light so shine that even other cultures are seeing the love that flows between My children.
Do not let it be only at this time of the year but continue to show forth My Light and My Love, each and everyday of your life.
My Love is already shed abroad in your heart by My Holy Spirit.
It is up to you to allow that love to come forth from you.
Love is a way of life.
It can be lived every minute of the day.
It will never fail you.
Trust in the Love for it is of Me.

Romans 12:10
Be kindly affectioned one to another with brotherly love in honor preferring one another.

DAILY ENCOURAGING WORDS...*TO LIVE BY*

December 25th

Arise and shine for the Glory Light of Jesus has come!
There is unity in My Church body when thy all come together and give Me praise as their Lord and Savior.
This happens on this day of the year all over the world.
It pleases Me so.
I see all My children in a joyful and peaceful state of mind and heart.
They look to others around them, and they see and put others first, instead of themselves.
This pleases Me so.
It brings Me joy, and much as it gives you joy.
Do not just do this for on day but develop this and do this everyday of the year, for this reason that I came and that I died on the Cross so that all that would believe in Me and what I did at Calvary for each and everyone in the world.
I AM Love and so do as you see Me do.
Spread My Love, Joy, and Peace wherever you go.

John 3:16
For God so loved the world, that He gave His only begotten Son that whosoever believeth in Him should not perish, but have everlasting life.

365 Day Devotional...God still speaks today...John 10:27

DAILY ENCOURAGING WORDS...*TO LIVE BY*

December 26th

Arise and shine for the Glory Light of Jesus has come!
Do you not see the difference between trusting in Me when things seem to go wrong then when you try to make things work on your own?
Your way of thinking in looking for ways to correct what is going on in your life will cause you grief.
Come to Me first and do not wait until things are way out of reach for you to work it out.
I AM your answer to fix the situation at hand.
Turn it all over to Me and believe that I will and can take care of it.
When you think you can do it, you are stepping over into pride and pride will only lead to destruction.
Everything falls apart and you are left wondering why it happened that way.
My child learn to put your trust totally in Me and bypass your way of thinking.

Psalm 145:18
The Lord is nigh unto all them that call upon Him, to all that call upon Him in truth.

DAILY ENCOURAGING WORDS...*TO LIVE BY*

December 27th

Arise and shine for the Glory Light of Jesus has come!
Take joy in the One who loves you and upholds you in the Palm of His Hand.
Take courage and praise and honor Me today!
As you walk in Me nothing can touch you.
There is peace, joy and love always living inside of you.
As you praise Me, you cause the love, joy, and peace to be activated inside of you to live for Me.
It is the Holy Spirit inside of you that helps you walk in the pathway I have put you on.
A path that will honor Me and cause you to have a glorious life.
So, trust Me and walk out your life and walk in the power of the Holy Spirit.
Be blessed this day My children.

Galatians 5:22
But the fruit of the Spirit is LOVE, JOY, PEACE, LONGSUFFERING, GENTLENESS, GOODNESS, FAITH, MEEKNESS: against there is no law.

DAILY ENCOURAGING WORDS...*TO LIVE BY*

December 28th

Arise and shine for the Glory Light of Jesus has come!
Look unto Me for everything that you need in your life.
I AM bringing you to a place in Me that you will be able to come to Me for everything.
You will depend on me and no other.
I AM your source and your only source.
Do not lean on the arm of man for they will fail you, for they do not have the whole counsel of God to direct you.
Your help cometh from your God, who knows all things.
When you depend on Me, you will have peace knowing that all is well in My Hands.
There is no fear of lack of anything for you are rooted and grounded in Me and My Word.
There is power in My Word.
This is why it is so important that you put My Word deep into your Spirit.
Cast everything on to Me and stand firm, believing that I will keep My Word.
Go about your day for you are blessed.

Psalm 55:22
Cast thy burden upon the Lord, and He shall sustain thee.
He shall never suffer the righteous to be moved.

DAILY ENCOURAGING WORDS...*TO LIVE BY*

December 29th

Arise and shine for the Glory Light of Jesus has come!
I want to bring you into a place in your walk with Me, where you will be able to put all your trust in Me.
It is a journey for you to walk through.
This journey starts with you surrendering all to Me and then putting your full trust in Me.
To be able to do the work in you, so you will be able to walk the way of life that I have planned out for you.
It is not your plans but My plans, that are much higher than what you can even think or imagine.
It is not only trusting Me, but it is about choosing by your own will to do what I have asked you to do.
I trusted mankind and put his own will in him, to make choices and I cannot cross man's will.
So, it is up to you what you want to do.
Choose to live a full and satisfying life, and you can do this by surrendering to Me and we will work and walk together.

Isaiah 55.8
For My thoughts, are not your thoughts, neither are your ways My ways saith the Lord.

DAILY ENCOURAGING WORDS...*TO LIVE BY*

December 30th

Arise and shine for the Glory Light of Jesus has come!
As you go into the New Year, decree, and declare what you want to happen in your life and your family's.
As I spoke at the beginning of creation, the Word was said and what I said came into being.
You have that same power with in you to do the same.
Remember what comes out of your mouth, (negative or positive) either way there is power to speak it into being.
Put a guard over your mouth before you speak over your life for the New Year.
My Holy Spirit is the power within you to speak forth and put in motion what you say.
I want to bless My children in the New Year.
They have not for they ask not.
Ask in faith of your desires, believing and then receiving.
Live in My presence and praise Me for the blessing that I will give to you.
Seek My face and not My Hand and expect Me to do what you have asked for.

Proverbs 18:21
Death and life are in the power of the tongue, and they that love it shall eat the fruit thereof.

DAILY ENCOURAGING WORDS...*TO LIVE BY*

December 31st

Arise and shine for the Glory Light of Jesus has come!
Walking in My Glory Light is the way that I designed it to be.
For I have given My Glory Light to every Born-Again person, that walks hand in Hand with Me.
My Glory Light is My very presence that lives within you by the Holy Spirit.
It is the resurrection power.
It is the power that will resurrect anything that is dead in your life.
Anything that you need done in your life, My presence will heal and make you whole.
There is nothing that I would not do for you, if only you would ask in Faith, believing and trusting in Me to do it.
For it is by Faith and your love walk that moves Me to work in your life.

John 8:12

Then spake Jesus again unto them, saying, I AM the Light of the world, he that followeth Me shall not walk in darkness, but shall have the light of life.

365 Day Devotional...God still speaks today...John 10:27

DAILY ENCOURAGING WORDS...*TO LIVE BY*

Prayer For Salvation & Receiving the Baptism Of The Holy Ghost.

Heavenly Father, I come to You in the Name of Jesus. Your Word says, "Whosoever shall call on the name of the Lord shall be saved" (Acts 2:21). I am calling on You. I pray and ask Jesus to come into my heart and be Lord over my life according to Romans 10:9-10: "If thou shalt confess with thy mouth the Lord Jesus, and shalt believe in thine heart that God hath raised him from the dead, thou shalt be saved. For with the heart man believeth unto righteousness; and with the mouth confession is made unto salvation." I do that now. I confess that Jesus is Lord, and I believe in my heart that God raised Him from the dead.

I am now reborn! I am a Christian—a child of Almighty God! I am saved! You also said in Your Word, "If ye then, being evil, know how to give good gifts unto your children: HOW MUCH MORE shall your heavenly Father give the Holy Spirit to them that ask him?" (Luke 11:13). I'm also asking You to fill me with the Holy Spirit. Holy Spirit, rise within me as I praise God. I fully expect to speak with other tongues as You give me the utterance (Acts 2:4). In Jesus' Name. Amen!

Begin to praise God for filling you with the Holy Spirit. Speak those words and syllables you receive—not in your own language, but the language given to you by the Holy Spirit. You must use your own voice. God will not force you to speak. Don't be concerned with how it sounds. It is a heavenly language!

Continue with the blessing God has given you and pray in the spirit every day. You are a born-again, Spirit-filled believer. You'll never be the same!

WELCOME into the KINGDOM OF GOD!

DAILY ENCOURAGING WORDS...*TO LIVE BY*

To order more copies of

DAILY ENCOURAGING WORDS...TO LIVE BY....

Refer to Kindle Books at Amazon.

ISBN 9798868483448

365 Day Devotional...God still speaks today...John 10:27

DAILY ENCOURAGING WORDS...*TO LIVE BY*

365 Day Devotional...God still speaks today...John 10:27

DAILY ENCOURAGING WORDS...*TO LIVE BY*

365 Day Devotional...God still speaks today...John 10:27

DAILY ENCOURAGING WORDS...*TO LIVE BY*

365 Day Devotional...God still speaks today...John 10:27

DAILY ENCOURAGING WORDS...*TO LIVE BY*

365 Day Devotional...God still speaks today...John 10:27

Manufactured by Amazon.ca
Acheson, AB